ESSAYS ON THE NEW DEAL

THE WALTER PRESCOTT WEBB MEMORIAL LECTURES: II

THE WALTER PRESCOTT WEBB MEMORIAL LECTURES

ESSAYS ON
THE NEW DEAL

BY

WILMON H. DROZE

GEORGE WOLFSKILL

WILLIAM E. LEUCHTENBURG

FOREWORD BY C. B. SMITH

Edited by
Harold M. Hollingsworth
and William F. Holmes

PUBLISHED FOR THE UNIVERSITY OF TEXAS AT ARLINGTON
BY THE UNIVERSITY OF TEXAS PRESS, AUSTIN & LONDON

ACKNOWLEDGMENT

"New Deal Critics: Did They Miss the Point?" is re-
printed with permission of The Macmillan Company
from *All but the People* by George Wolfskill. Copyright
© by George Wolfskill and John A. Hudson, 1969.

Standard Book Number 292–78410–4
Library of Congress Catalog Card Number 73–80898
Copyright © 1969 by The University of Texas at Arlington
All Rights Reserved
Type set by G&S Typesetters, Austin
Printed by The Steck-Warlick Company, Austin
Bound by Universal Bookbindery, Inc., San Antonio

FOREWORD

These three essays on the New Deal era, presented by professional historians at the second series of the Walter Prescott Webb Memorial Lectures, speak for themselves both interestingly and effectively. They highlight the fact that much of the current social and economic philosophy accepted at all governmental levels had its origins in the New Deal years. While still controversial in some circles, the subject matter contained in these essays does not draw the fiery criticism it would have drawn a few years ago. With the passing of time and with acknowledged changes in attitude—particularly within the American middle-class population —there is the feeling that the New Deal led to a significant improvement in educational and economic opportunities for many segments of the American people. Therefore, a discussion of the New Deal is significant and timely, particularly for those of the past two generations, those generations which are (or soon will be) giving direction to this nation's way of life.

The influence of Walter Prescott Webb is in some respects like that of the New Deal: it is a continuing process. In his introduction to the first volume of the Webb Lecture Series, Professor E. C. Barksdale, head of the Department of History and Philosophy of The University of Texas at Arlington, added significantly to our understanding of Walter Prescott Webb as an intellectual, a historian, and a man; he also indicated some of the dimensions of his influence. The Webb Lecture Series can and should be a continuing tribute to Webb's memory. But few friends of Webb would argue that this Memorial Series should be the sole vehicle for developing his ideas, for finishing the work he left unfinished, for realizing the Webb dream.

I I

To the historian—and to a larger reading public than some would expect—it may not be necessary to prove the case of Webb's high professional rank and status. But, since proof is required in courthouses and academic circles, I shall offer some evidence of Webb's greatness through the testimony of historians, editors, and others.

Arnold J. Toynbee, in his Introduction to Webb's *The Great Frontier*, wrote of him: "Being, as he was, a thinker whose mind never stopped producing new thoughts, Walter Prescott Webb became a historian of a kind that is not very common in our time. He managed to combine mastery of a special area of history with a vision of the total history of the world." Toynbee said of *The Great Frontier* that "the central idea amounts to a new theory of the Western World since 1492."

In an informal tribute written after Webb had died in a highway accident, J. Frank Dobie, the well-known author of books on the Southwest, said: "His superiority as a historian lies in his perception, his power of thought, his mastery of language, his interpretations of the land and the ever-evolving currents of human affairs." The tribute concludes with these words:

Any man who has seen and been a part of life wants to leave it before decomposing into a juiceless vegetable. Webb died standing up, as Caesar considered it meet for a man to die. In a flash he passed from wisdom and happiness to the finality of death. No person who has added as much to the heritage of human life as Walter Webb added ceases to be. His thinking, his writing, and his standing up will surely continue as elements of his projected shadow.

Dobie and others placed emphasis on the diversity of Webb's ideas. His writing on non-historical subjects, including *More Water for Texas* and *Flat Top: A Story of Modern Ranching*, and his numerous essays—sometimes humorous, sometimes thought-provoking, usually both—affirmed his catholic tastes. Rupert N. Richardson, the author of *Texas, the Lone Star State*, said of Webb that he was "interested in ideas and was a genius at developing them. To him facts meant nothing unless one was able to discover their meaning. It was with this point of view that he became a great historian."

John Fischer, while editor of *Harper's*, praised Webb for his belief that history was inexorably a part of literature; that a historian had an obligation, a moral duty, to express his ideas and convictions in a straightforward manner—and to write well. Wilson Hudson, professor of English at The University of Texas at Austin, said, "No small part of the merit of *The Great Frontier* is its directness, simplicity, and clarity of expression."

Sometimes Webb's ideas were expressed with more than directness, simplicity, clarity; sometimes they were served up with disarming bluntness. Professor Joe B. Frantz, a colleague in the History Department of The University of Texas at Austin, was as close to Webb as any man. Frantz has quoted Webb on politics as saying, "I believe in a strong Republican Party, but not strong enough to win—only to keep the Democrats honest."

And on another occasion Webb asked, "What did the Republican Party ever do for Texas?"

In Webb's family background and in his own household there was the constant pressure of adherence to the traditions of the Old South. But Webb's position was, "Let the dead past bury its dead," and "Lift up thine eyes to the Western horizon." As late as the 1960's, members of Webb's immediate family were distressed by the choice of name for a new luxury hotel in Houston —the Sheraton-Lincoln. Webb found this most amusing. But this kind of influence did not shake his own views. "He went into the state of Mississippi," Frantz relates, "and told the local citizenry at Oxford that the state was plain stupid if it permitted its historic adherence to racial segregation to bar its material progress."

Webb's international popularity and greatness were emphasized in England by his teaching performance at London University and Oxford. (And an example of his business acumen was also revealed in his London visit by the purchase of a painting of a buffalo stampede, a painting which he later sold at a twenty-five hundred per cent profit.) Former President Lyndon B. Johnson sought and received Webb's counsel and demonstrated his regard for the man in different ways, including writing the Foreword to the second edition of *The Texas Rangers*.

III

Webb undoubtedly reached his widest audience in 1961 when the July issue of *Harper's* and the August issue of *Reader's Digest* carried the story of "The Search for William E. Hinds." Two separate reprints, each with appropriate comments from

Texas members of the United States Congress, subsequently appeared in the *Congressional Record*. It is estimated that this unusual and heart-warming story may have been read by more than twenty million people.

The Webb-Hinds relationship resulted from a letter written by Webb to a youth magazine, *The Sunny South*, wherein he stated his interest in obtaining the kind of education that would enable him to become a teacher and writer. Hinds read Webb's letter in the magazine and responded with encouragement and an offer of financial assistance. From 1904 to the fall of 1914, when Hinds died, Webb was able to use a line of credit with Hinds of up to $500 in pursuit of his ambitious objectives. During this period Webb was forced to drop out of college and teach in order to take care of the needs of his family. Although Webb very much wanted to meet his benefactor face to face, he was unable to do so.

The Hinds-Webb relationship inspired one of Webb's University of Texas Graduate School students, class of 1928, to undertake a special project using reprints of the *Harper's* story. This project, begun in September of 1961, included the mailing of two thousand reprints to friends of The University of Texas scattered over the United States. Although the covering letter with the reprints solicited no comments or reply, over three hundred acknowledgements were received, along with praise and cash gifts for Webb. This money became a part of the Webb-Hinds Scholarship Fund of The University of Texas at Austin.

In a letter of September 22, 1961, Webb wrote:

> The Hinds story has brought so many letters from all over the world that about two hundred of them are still unanswered. . . .

I have already seen evidence that they are bringing results to the University. . . . I really do not have much modesty about the Hinds story as I proved by laying bare before the public something very personal. It was not an easy thing to do, I couldn't have done it much earlier, but I did it at exactly the right time.

On another occasion Webb stated, "The Webb-Hinds Memorial Fund is now set up, and it will grow. The first contributor lives in Connecticut, said he is a 'damn' Yankee and asked that it be spelled in two words." I reminded Webb that William E. Hinds was also a "damn Yankee" and that I rated him pretty high. Concerning what he had been able to learn about Hinds, Webb wrote, "There is not much personal information about him, only three or four people ever saw him, and none of them really knew him. The real William E. Hinds I found in the generous spirit of the American people."

In a letter of December 11, 1961, Webb had something to say about another, related matter close to his heart, that of university graduates' interesting themselves in their alma mater:

It has been my observation that it is the boys who had a rather tough time getting through the University who have the most affection for it. Many seem to feel that what the University did for them was nothing exceptional, and that they really owe no obligation to it. I have often wondered why it is that in the Ivy League, the graduates shower down gifts each year and make generous bequests. Is it something we of the faculty do, or fail to do, that makes the rank and file of our graduates so indifferent?

In the last paragraph he added: "The University has given me a great deal, not only what passes for an education, but an opportunity to do the sort of work I most wanted to do. I am glad I am in position to do something in return. My own life, though rather hard in the early years, has grown richer as I have gone along, and here lately it has become very rich indeed."

David Shanks, a former Austin *American* editor and a friend of Webb's, described the unusual Hinds-Webb relationship with an air of mysticism and hope:

Walter Prescott Webb's acknowledgement of his obligation to William E. Hinds has come to be an inspiration of sorts to all those of us who feel that we are in some way obligated to humanity but are uncertain that humanity ever will benefit in fact from our contribution. Walter Webb's search for Mr. Hinds is important because it reaffirms the possibility (hopefully a probability) that one man can directly assist another and that the recipient will continue through a succeeding generation the good traits of humanity.

Walter Webb's publicly conducted search for the man he never knew face-to-face causes acknowledgement of the personal obligation to Hinds to transcend the restricted limits of a personal relationship, debt and debtor, giver and recipient. This simply is not adequate to describe the flow of results stemming from a personal arrangement. In short this is another of those events which are described best as an American Epic.

Why is this so?

The Webb-Hinds relation was improbably begun. So random was the chance of it occurring at all that when it did, there was an appeal to the drama of the event that can be appreciated only now.

Not only was this relationship improbable, once it had occurred, the odds of succeeding were so staggering that it should not have happened.

A large part of this saga is that unrecorded aspect of Dr. Webb's own determination to help others as he had been helped.

I V

At the time of his fatal automobile accident, Webb's friends knew that his mission in life had not been fulfilled. He had more to do, much more; and there should be a sense of guilt and remorse in some of us for having made so little real effort to see that his mission was fulfilled.

What was left undone? Arnold Toynbee, for example, has said that Webb "could have produced a third great theory." Close friends were well aware of Webb's desire to found a school for historians. He also wanted to assemble a select team of historians and scholars to reinterpret the history of the United States in the light of changes, particularly changes since the nineteen thirties, and then to write of it. Webb wanted to revise his *Texas Rangers* and add a second volume covering their recent history. Conservation, specifically water and grass conservation, along with their by-products, was a near obsession with Webb. He loved the land. And he would have made further contributions in this field which he considered so critical to the future welfare of America and the world.

Active and influential on University of Texas faculty committees concerned with the College of Arts and Sciences, Webb had sought the realization of long-range goals:

(1) To improve teaching and learning through the use of scientific and technical equipment such as radio, television, and computers;

(2) To give the College of Arts and Sciences greater importance and prestige in preparing the student for his final vocation

(to Webb the role of the arts and sciences in developing the student to think, to communicate, to organize his knowledge and associate it with the humanities was of prime importance in the eventual success of the student in the business and professional world); and

(3) To hasten the elevation of The University of Texas from the academic "bush league" into real competition with the great universities of the country.

What, then, are we to do to make the Webb dream a reality? March 8, 1969 was the sixth anniversary of the passing of Walter Prescott Webb. Somebody somewhere should be making plans for realizing that dream. Focusing public attention and acclaim upon an academician may seem to some a useless occupation. But we hope there are others who will "put their pocketbook where their mouth is," as Webb said in reference to money he put into the Hinds-Webb scholarship fund. Plans and money. These are the necessary ingredients for properly honoring one who did so much for Texas, for the nation, for the world.

PREFACE

This volume presents the second annual Walter Prescott Webb
Memorial Lectures. They were delivered at the Theater Building
of The University of Texas at Arlington, April 5, 1967. Following the pattern of the preceding year, two of the lecturers were
members of the faculty of The University of Texas at Arlington,
the third was a distinguished visiting historian.

In his lecture Wilmon Droze temporarily deserted his investigations of the Tennessee Valley Authority to chronicle the development of the New Deal's Shelterbelt Program. George
Wolfskill moved beyond his analysis of the American Liberty
League to evaluate the relevance of the criticism heaped upon
Roosevelt by all segments of American life. William Leuchtenburg of Columbia University concluded the lectures with a bril-
liant synthesis of Roosevelt's Court Packing Plan.

To one who is unfamiliar with the history of The University
of Texas at Arlington it may seem strange that this institution
should memorialize Walter P. Webb with this annual series of
lectures, but Webb had close and enduring connections with this
campus. Arlington came into the educational system of the state
of Texas as a junior college headed by Dean E. E. Davis, who,
coincidentally, had roomed with Webb when they were both
students in Austin. Through the years Webb repeatedly asserted
that this institution had a bright future and during its infancy

used his influence to direct able young scholars into its faculty. He followed its growth in size and its elevation to full college rank with the peculiar interest of a man seeing his prophesies fulfilled. We can only regret that an automobile accident prevented his seeing it bear the name of the institution which he served and which served him so well throughout his adult life.

HAROLD M. HOLLINGSWORTH
WILLIAM F. HOLMES

Arlington, Texas

CONTENTS

ESSAYS ON THE NEW DEAL

The New Deal's Shelterbelt Project
1934-1942

⌧⌧⌧

BY WILMON H. DROZE

ON JULY 21, 1934, while President Franklin D. Roosevelt was cruising in Hawaiian waters, White House officials announced what became the most ridiculed undertaking of the New Deal era—the shelterbelt project. Shortly after the overdramatic and oversimplified White House statement, Secretary of Agriculture Henry A. Wallace and Chief Forester Ferdinand A. Silcox released greater details of the venture. They revealed that the shelterbelt would be a hundred miles wide, reach from Canada to Texas, and cost approximately $75,000,000 over a decade. The shelterbelt zone was to consist of forested strips seven rods in width (132 feet) located one mile apart. The stretches would be planted along north-south lines. Each strip would contain seventeen to twenty-one rows of trees. Each two rows would be planted with different species of trees. Forester Silcox pointed out that the tree belts would ameliorate drought conditions, protect crops and livestock, reduce dust storms, and provide relief to the residents of the drought-stricken area.

A hot and dust-plagued nation received the news of the New Deal's latest weapon in the battle to save the soil—the shelterbelt —with mixed emotions. Feelings ranged from fear to joy, and expressions of doubt, consternation, and skepticism were everywhere. A forestry expert said that "no sooner had the project been announced than foresters took sides."[1] Many of the nation's editors considered the venture of dubious value and possibly ungodly! Some observed that "only God can make a tree . . . that if He had wanted a forest on the windscoured prairies of Nebraska and Kansas, He would have put it there . . . and that for FDR to rush in where the Almighty had feared to tread was not only silly, but possibly blasphemous."[2] Professors in the forestry schools of the country "were more than skeptical, they were inimical,"[3] said a shelterbelt official. R. E. Karper, vice director of Texas A&M's Experiment Station at College Station, Texas, informed the editor of the *Journal of Forestry* that "we consider the project . . . exceedingly questionable."[4]

While the nation's intelligentsia were dissecting the plan, farmers of North Dakota, South Dakota, Nebraska, Kansas, Oklahoma, and Texas—where the belt was to be located—waited, worried, and mused. The press had so confused them that many of them had the impression that the President planned to estab-

[1] E. N. Munns and J. H. Stoeckeler, "How Are the Great Plains Shelterbelts?" *Journal of Forestry*, XLIV (April, 1946), 237.

[2] Arthur H. Carhart, "Shelterbelts: A 'Failure' That Didn't Happen," *Harper's Magazine*, CCXXI (October, 1960), 74–75.

[3] Raphael Zon, "The Hydrologic and Climatic Influence of the Forest Is Basic to the Concept of Forestry," *Journal of Forestry*, XLIX (December, 1951), 882.

[4] H. H. Chapman, "The Shelterbelt Project," *Journal of Forestry*, XXXII (December, 1934), 965.

lish a solid forested zone a thousand miles long and a hundred miles wide along the hundredth meridian! Other cultivators did not want trees because their presence on the farm usually meant stump removal and other unpleasant tasks. Some farmers just knew that trees would not grow on the prairies; consequently, the whole idea was obviously a wasteful one. Still other lords of the soil favored the erection of water-impoundment devices as a more desirable way of using relief money. To most, the endeavor just seemed too much like some sort of rain-making scheme at a time when they were in desperate need of a comprehensive program of relief, a need which had arisen out of prolonged economic dislocation and searing droughts. Clearly, the Forest Service had a major selling job to do if the project was to win the support of the plainsmen.

If foresters, forestry professors, and farmers were concerned about the shelterbelt plan, imagine the consternation of economy-minded Republicans and Democrats over the enterprise. An Indiana Democrat told his colleagues in the House of Representatives that "this whole scheme was fairly dripping with extravagance."[5] To many politicos, the idea of spending $75,000,000 in an area where few voters lived and for a project of uncertain merits was politically unwise, grossly unfair, and hardly in keeping with their promises to balance the budget. Moreover, some congressional proponents of a drought relief program found it difficult to accept Chief Forester Silcox's contention that the tree belts would "ameliorate the effects of weather on a large scale."[6] To most

[5] *Congressional Record*, 74 Cong. 2 Sess., p. 2716.

[6] E. L. Perry, "History of the Prairie States Forestry Project" (Typescript copy in files of Rocky Mountain Forest and Range Experiment Station, Lincoln, Nebraska).

congressmen the President's plan to afforest the prairies was extravagant, impractical, and certain to be wasteful.

As the shelterbelt plan was losing its headline quality, its sponsor, the Forest Service of the Department of Agriculture, was busily attempting to implement the presidential order of July, 1934. The shelterbelt scheme was neither a whim nor an overnight development to win the farm vote in 1934, as some insisted at the time.[7] The idea had received the attention of the President and several of the bureaus of the Department of Agriculture for more than a year prior to its disclosure. Apparently the idea originated with President Roosevelt when his train was derailed near Butte, Montana, in September, 1932. The denuded hillsides upon which he gazed, made barren of vegetation by copper-smelting operations, led him to inquire into the possibility of planting the treeless areas of the "Great American Desert," as he referred to the Great Plains.[8] After the campaign and election of 1932, and the hectic Hundred Days of early 1933, the President, in August, 1933, returned to his idea of planting the plains and requested the Forest Service to determine the technical and economic feasibility of such a venture.[9] The disclosure a year later indicated that the foresters believed that the prairie plains would grow trees and that they were ready to try.

The time for such a venture was ripe, for "black blizzards" were sweeping the prairies and bringing red rain to states along

[7] Jonathan Mitchell, "Shelter Belt Realities," *New Republic*, XXC (August 29, 1934), 69–70.

[8] Munns and Stoekeler, "How Are the Great Plains Shelterbelts?" p. 237.

[9] Edgar B. Nixon (ed.), *Franklin D. Roosevelt and Conservation, 1911–1945* (Hyde Park: General Services Administration, National Archives and Records, Franklin D. Roosevelt Library, 1957), I, 198–199.

the eastern seaboard. The duststorms dramatized the need for erosion controls and made the problem of relief in the prairie states more acute. Finally, nursery stock would have to be developed well in advance of any planting activity; thus, by late summer the foresters urged the inauguration of the venture immediately or another year would be required to initiate the scheme.[10] Clearly, several forces came into focus to bring about the dramatic news of July 21, 1934.

At the time of the project's announcement the foresters were agreed upon the technical and economic feasibility of the idea but upon little else. On August 2, 1934, at a summit meeting attended by Secretary of Agriculture Henry A. Wallace, Undersecretary of Agriculture Rexford G. Tugwell, Chief Forester Ferdinand A. Silcox, and other high-ranking officials of the Forest Service, policies were discussed and plans were made for launching the enterprise. Project organization was established. Two directors were named: Fred W. Morrell became Administrative Director and Raphael Zon was named Technical Director. Both were career foresters. Morrell's assignment lasted only a few weeks, and he was replaced by the associate administrative head, Paul H. Roberts, who remained as Director for the life of the project. Lincoln, Nebraska, was chosen as the administrative headquarters of the enterprise while the Lakes States Experiment Station at St. Paul, Minnesota, served as the technical center of the venture.[11]

[10] *Ibid.*, pp. 319–320; Avis D. Carlson, "Dust Blowing," *Harper's Magazine*, CLXXI (July, 1935), 149–158; "The Soil and Civilization," *Nature Magazine*, XXVI (July, 1935), 43–45.

[11] Perry, "Prairie States Forestry Project," pp. 28–29; "Morrell and Zon Head Shelterbelt Project," *American Forests*, XL (September, 1934), 415.

Many highly important problems were left unresolved by the delegates to the August meeting. For example, no decision was made about whether the tree belts would be planted on government or on privately owned lands. Interestingly, Tugwell suggested that the government purchase a solid block of land a hundred miles wide from Texas to Canada and plant it in grass or trees! Tugwell's proposal had resulted from another complication, that of how to utilize the sum of $10,000,000 which had been allocated to the endeavor by the President from the Emergency Relief Act of June, 1934. This difficulty was soon resolved by the Comptroller-General. Lastly, several technical problems emerged involving delicate political considerations which demanded further refinement. The most complex issues were those concerning land ownership and the source of the young trees; that is, should the seedlings be grown in privately owned or governmentally controlled nurseries? The latter issue would significantly influence the project's history.[12]

Action followed the conference of the shelterbelt leaders. By August 8, 1934, personnel began to arrive at the Lincoln, Nebraska, office. Suddenly all activity ceased. Comptroller-General John R. McCarl, one of Harding's better appointees, refused to release funds allocated to the project by the President's order.[13] A budget crisis brought the venture to a halt. McCarl, who apparently delighted in holding up funds for some New Deal projects,[14] contended that the Relief Act required that appropriated

---

[12] Nixon, *Roosevelt and Conservation*, I, 328–329; Perry, "Prairie States Forestry Project," pp. 28–30.

[13] Nixon, *Roosevelt and Conservation*, I, 324–329.

[14] Elliott Roosevelt (ed.), *F. D. R.: His Personal Letters, 1928–1945* (New York: Duell, Sloan and Pearce, 1950), I, 515.

funds be spent for projects which brought immediate relief, whereas the benefits from the shelterbelt would not be obtained for years. He also affirmed that Congress should have the right to examine the merits of the venture before any money was expended for it. McCarl's objection to the presidential allotment brought a series of hurried conferences between Roosevelt, Secretary of the Treasury Henry Morgenthau, Jr., and himself.[15] The conferees decided that an allocation of $1,000,000 might be made for preliminary work which would give immediate relief to many unemployed.

Late in September, 1934, funds for the project were made available to the Forest Service. Forester Silcox explicitly and comprehensively outlined for Project Director Paul H. Roberts the program that was to be implemented. Roberts was directed to proceed with vigor and enthusiasm and to win political support for the scheme at the grassroots level. He was told to collaborate with Technical Director Zon in collecting all manner of data to assure greater acceptability in scientific and political circles. To pacify the nursery interests, Roberts was instructed to lease rather than to purchase nursery sites. To obtain the broadest political base possible, the Director was urged to create tree belts in all six of the prairie states and to plant as widely within each of the states as personnel, work facilities, and the availability of planting stock and funds would permit. Roberts was commanded to do more than to plant trees with the funds. He was enjoined to embark upon a program of construction of water and soil conservation devices to provide water for the trees. Silcox told Roberts to refrain from purchasing any land for planting sites, but to include an option to purchase in all cooperative agreements made

[15] Nixon, *Roosevelt and Conservation*, I, 324–329.

with the farmers. The Chief Forester then provided a tentative division of the $1,000,000 budget which earmarked the majority of the money for lease agreement fees, surveys for sites, and nursery operations. These guidelines, although refashioned somewhat by changing conditions and experiences, governed the project in the future.[16]

The Silcox directive was carefully drawn to assure the project's survival. He cautiously tried to formulate a program that would placate the plan's enemies and win friends for the endeavor from as large an area as possible. He knew that the project had to be removed from the realm of the ridiculous where a large portion of the public and the press had placed it. Scientific and political respectability were essential to winning financial support from Congress. Success in obtaining congressional approval carried rich rewards with it, for success would bring a new opportunity for the Forest Service—plains forestry. Planting the treeless prairies and selected areas of the plains offered the Service an unlimited opportunity to become a major New Deal conservation agency in a region where the Forest Service was largely unknown. The Forester was optimistic in the fall of 1934; therefore, he informed his subordinates at Lincoln to plan for large-scale operations after July 1, 1935, the start of the next fiscal year, when congressional approval and support could be expected.[17]

During the fall and winter of 1934–1935, extensive exploration of the climate, soils, natural vegetation, existing windbreaks, and agricultural conditions in the prairie states were conducted. The additional data brought some revisions in thought. The

[16] Perry, "Prairie States Forestry Project," pp. 30–32.
[17] *Ibid.*, pp. 30–31.

hundred-mile-wide shelterbelt zone was moved slightly eastward, and its boundaries were fixed. It was to extend fifty miles each side of a center line following the ninety-ninth meridian from the northern North Dakota border to a point in central Kansas. At that point the center line would move southwestwardly through Mangum, Oklahoma, until it reached Childress, Texas, the extreme southern terminal of the belt. The western edge of the zone would coincide with a line of average annual rainfall of fifteen inches in the northern prairie plains and the twenty-two-inch line in the Southwest. The eastern border of the zone, fifty miles east of the centerline, was an area where no special efforts for tree growing were needed. The outer limits of the belt followed county lines—a factor that caused ill will later, when project proponents were asked to explain why trees could be grown in one county and could not be grown across the county line in an adjacent county! One Oklahoma congressman fought the project for several years because his home county was not included within the shelterbelt zone. Eventually these unrealistic borders were abandoned in favor of scientific determinants as to the edges of the region. Before the venture was terminated, belts were planted from the ninety-sixth to the hundredth meridian.[18]

As planting time approached in 1935, project leaders from state and local shelterbelt administrative units met with the headquarters forces at Lincoln, Nebraska. Director Roberts opened the session with a challenge to his subordinates to join in a crusade of tree planting. He urged:

[18] Raymond G. Carroll, "Shelterbelt," *Saturday Evening Post*, CCVIII (October 5, 1935), 23, 81–83; Raphael Zon, "Shelterbelts—Futile Dreams or Workable Plan," *Science*, XXCI (April 26, 1935), 391–394; Perry, "Prairie States Forestry Project," pp. 24, 34–35.

I am impressed by the responsibility we must assume. We are attacking the problem of growing trees on a scale of great magnitude, not in a region where successful tree planting can be taken for granted, but by deliberate choice in a zone at about the climatic limits of tree growth. It would be difficult to conceive of a more intriguing enterprise or of one which offers a greater challenge to the ingenuity and skill of an organization. We are, furthermore, not alone concerned with tree planting. The Project has far broader phases. It is, in its present proportions, a new departure in forestry.[19]

The ringing address was followed by two days of discussion in which the delegates considered land tenure arrangements, planting and nursery policies, field operations, fiscal control, and public relations matters. The February, 1935, meeting marked the zenith of Forest Service hopes for a comprehensive program of plains forestry. Thereafter, technical decision-making gave way more and more to political considerations in the formulation of project policies as the venture sought to survive in a sea of criticism made even rougher by limited financing.[20]

For the moment, though, the lean times were yet to come, and in the meantime the foresters had seedlings to plant. During the fall and winter months of 1934–1935, shelterbelt field forces had been busy collecting seeds and wilding stock, developing seedlings in the nurseries, and negotiating with private nurseries to buy their planting stock if suitable. Other workers were in the field surveying, selecting, determining soil conditions, and leasing

[19] Perry, "Prairie States Forestry Project," p. 33.
[20] *Congressional Record*, 74 Cong. 2 Sess., p. 2878; 77 Cong. 1 Sess., pp. A–1681–1682, A–1846, A–2980; 75 Cong. 3 Sess., pp. 8584–8585.

the planting sites. At first, yearly rentals were based on the productive value of the land. After July 1, 1935, the Agricultural Adjustment Administration worked out an arrangement so that the land devoted to shelterbelt plantings would be accepted as crop-reduction acreage by the AAA. When the AAA was declared illegal by the courts in January, 1936, a simple cooperative agreement was made between the farmer and the Forest Service whereby the government furnished the stock and maintained the plantings until the end of that fiscal year on June 30, 1936. The farmer, in turn, provided the land, fenced the belt, and prepared the land for planting. Costs between the two, the government and the individual landowner, were equally divided. Before the arrangements were made with the AAA at the end of the first planting season, the foresters were hard-pressed to obtain enough planting sites. Plains farmers were not sold on the tree belt idea. Many refused to participate in the program because they doubted its soundness, and others did not want to take land out of production. Eventually, however, enough sites were found to plant most of the seedlings which had been gathered that fall and winter.[21]

On March 18, 1935, the first tree of the first shelterbelt was planted on a farm near Mangum, Oklahoma. Planting in Oklahoma continued for the next month, and when the season ended, approximately fourteen miles of belts had been established. The belts averaged a half mile in length, were about 132 feet wide, and contained seventeen to twenty-one rows of trees that ranged in height from eighteen inches to two feet. Each belt included eight to ten different species of trees. Taller-growing hardwoods were planted in the center rows. On each side of the hardwoods

[21] Perry, "Prairie States Forestry Project," pp. 36–41.

rows of evergreens were established. On the outer rows, low shrubs were installed to trap snows and to ward off weeds and assorted prairie varmints. Most of the early plantings were placed on east-west lines to counter the hot summer winds from the south and wintry blasts from the northwest.[22]

The tree types utilized in the belts varied from state to state. Some varieties such as green ash, American and Chinese elms, post oak, cottonwood, and ponderosa pine were planted in all six states of the zone. Once the belt was completed it then had to be fenced to protect the trees from cattle, and the young seedlings had to be treated with poison to deter rodents and insects. Finally, each strip had to be cultivated several times to prevent undergrowth from sapping the moisture from the soil. If properly planted and cared for, the trees would, when mature, form a triangular-shaped dike that would deflect the winds upward and over a horizontal distance ten to twenty times the heights of the trees. Thus, with the velocity of the wind reduced, soil movement and desiccation would be decreased. The result of such actions would be moisture conservation for crop use.[23]

The planting of the Oklahoma belts represented only a small portion of the 1935 effort. Planting was begun in Kansas on March 19, in Nebraska on April 4, and in the Dakotas later that month. Texas was tardy in organizing its state unit, but the Oklahoma field forces came south and planted two short strips. By June 7, 1935, all planting activity had been completed. The season's action had resulted in the establishment of 125 miles of tree strips comprising 2,500 acres on 232 farms, and required al-

22 *Ibid.*, pp. 40–43; Carroll, "Shelterbelt," pp. 23, 81–83.
23 *Ibid.*

most two million trees. Some twenty-nine species had been used throughout the zone.[24]

The first planting season was a stern test for the project's staff. In the first place, the tree-planting activities were under constant public scrutiny. Ceremonials were held in some localities at the installation of the first trees. The public and press maintained a continuous watch to see if the trees were going to live. The weather gave the planters considerable misery. In the northern plains rain fell during most of the planting season, while in the south, drought, dust storms, and rains interrupted the work several times. Drought conditions in the southern part of the zone forced the foresters to water some of the evergreens for the first and only time. Wind-driven sandstorms provided some trouble, for they sand-cleaned the rodent-control mixture from the tree trunks and set the stage for forays against the trees by prairie rodents.

The first experience in the field taught the shelterbelt staff many lessons. Among the things learned were: that a number two round-pointed, long-handled shovel was an ideal planting tool, that direct seeding of land was valueless, that a ten-to-sixteen-man crew made the most efficient planting unit, and that methods successfully utilized in one state or area might be quite unsuitable in another. In the review of the season's work, most progress reports contained long lists of suggestions for future use. A project officer asserted that "the 1935 planting season was

[24] *The New York Times*, June 23, 1935; Carroll, "Shelterbelt," pp. 23, 81–83, 85; U. S. Department of Agriculture, Prairie States Forestry Project, *Annual Planting Accomplishment Reports*, 1935–1942 (in files of Rocky Mountain Forest and Range Experiment Station, Lincoln, Nebraska).

the most significant that the project ever experienced. It was there that a multitude of experiments were carried out and that many of the basic principles which later guided the project were discovered."[25]

While foresters and farmers were planting trees, technical forces headquartered at the Lakes States Experiment Station were learning more about planting the prairies. The massive research effort launched in the fall of 1934 began to culminate in report form in 1935. In a lengthy report entitled *Possibilities of Shelterbelt Planting in the Plains Region* and submitted to the President late in 1935, the technical staff provided a blueprint for a plains forestry program. The document served three purposes. It gathered together and digested all previous research on growing trees on the plains; it provided scientific support for the tree belt idea; and it served as a technical guide for the field forces. The blueprint was highly regarded in both scientific and forestry circles. It established the idea, at least theoretically, that trees could be grown on the plains if the proper species of trees were selected and given care and protection.[26]

Establishing the scientific feasibility of the shelterbelts was just one of the accomplishments of the technical staff. Its other successes included the development of several methods of coping with the wily prairie hare, who found the young trees savory provender. Drives were conducted, often with WPA labor, and poisons were provided to the farmers. Achieving grasshopper

[25] Perry, "Prairie States Forestry Project," p. 44.

[26] U. S. Department of Agriculture, Lakes States Forest Experiment Station, *Possibilities of Shelterbelt Planting in the Plains Region* (Washington: Government Printing Office, 1935); Perry, "Prairie States Forestry Project," pp. 44–46, 50–51.

control was another essential accomplishment of the scientists. Studies of wind action and wind control and the planting of experimental belts were other research activities of the technical group. One unique achievement of both the technical and field forces was the perfection of a tree-planting machine. It was not used until the coming of World War II created a labor scarcity, for the shelterbelt project was partially a make-work venture. When needed, though, in 1942, the machine made it possible to complete the planting season with fewer workers. The contraption could plant eight thousand trees during an eight-hour day. Finally, the magnitude of the task assigned to the forestry scientists is indeed worthy of comment. In addition to the above-mentioned attainments, the researchers had to determine the proper species of trees for a region that extended through sixteen degrees of latitude, to make hundreds of soil surveys of the tree-growing capabilities of many kinds of soils, and to prescribe the specialized care for the numerous varieties of young trees that were planted throughout the long zone. Survival rates of 70 to 80 per cent for the seedlings attest to the effectiveness of their efforts.[27]

Although the mastery of the technology of growing trees on the prairies was an important attainment, a second difficulty now awaited the foresters—that of convincing Congress that it should give financial support to the idea. From the project's beginning, members of Congress had expressed doubts about the wisdom of it. Therefore, considerable energy was expended to create a new image of the enterprise. The report, *Possibilities of Shelterbelt*

---

[27] Perry, "Prairie States Forestry Project, pp. 50–53; Jerome Dahl, "Progress and Development of the Prairie States Forestry Project," *Journal of Forestry,* XXXVIII (April, 1946), 301–306.

Planting in the Plains Region, was one weapon in the battle for congressional and public acceptance. The planting program of 1935 was shaped to secure certain political objectives.[28] The intensive care given the seedlings to assure maximum survival and the selection of planting sites in all six of the plains states were efforts to widen the scheme's political base. Finally, the sacrificing of the unusually broad program originally planned by Chief Forester Silcox and his subordinates, after Comptroller-General McCarl questioned the legality of the use of relief funds for the venture, was indeed a political retreat. Clearly, the strong opposition to the project convinced the leaders of the Forest Service that they would have to make concessions to the opponents of the idea.

During the first two years of the program's life, funds for the project came from emergency relief appropriations. President Roosevelt had allocated $1,000,000 to it in 1934, from the Drought Relief Act of that year. As the next fiscal year approached, from July 1, 1935, to June 30, 1936, a second allocation of almost two million dollars was made to the project from the unemployment relief sum administered by the newly-created Works Progress Administration. A direct outlay from Congress was not sought in 1935 because the stigma of illegality attached to the scheme by McCarl still remained and because the Forest Service had not yet marshalled its evidence to show the scientific soundness of the plan. Moreover, the endeavor had not won public acceptance by 1935.[29]

---

[28] "Shelterbelt Project Hits Snag," *American Forests,* XL (October, 1934), 478; *Congressional Record,* 74 Cong. 2 Sess., pp. 2941–2944, 8399–8441; Perry, "Prairie States Forestry Project," pp. 30–31.

[29] W. I. Drummond, "Dust Bowl," *Review of Reviews,* XCIII (June,

When the second session of the Seventy-fourth Congress convened in January, 1936, the Forest Service made its bid for congressional authorization and an appropriation. The President's budget for the fiscal year 1937 allowed a sum of $1,000,000 for the project. In the Senate, under the guiding hand of Senator George Norris of Nebraska, the appropriation item survived both the Senate Appropriations Committee and floor debate. In the House, though, the request ran into stiff opposition. The House Appropriations Committee and its subcommittee eliminated the request from the appropriations bill. Not a single committee member supported the shelterbelt appropriation during the hearings. On the House floor, Representative Phil Ferguson, from the western part of Oklahoma, sought to amend the appropriations bill and to provide the amount necessary to continue the nursery operations. He hoped to protect the young seedlings, but his proposal was rejected by a vote of three to one. Finally, the sheer folly of allowing 60,000,000 nursery seedlings to go to waste moved the House and Senate conferees to grant a sum of $170,000 for the project. This money was approved with the understanding that it would be used to liquidate the venture once and forever.[30]

1936), 37–40; Wilson Compton, "Government Versus Desert: The Fallacy of the Shelter Belt," *Forum*, XCIII (April, 1935), 237–239; Anna L. Reisch, "Franklin D. Roosevelt and Conservation," (unpublished doctoral dissertation, University of Wisconsin, Madison, 1952), pp. 203, 291–293; *Congressional Record*, 74 Cong. 2 Sess., pp. 2895–2896, 2941–2944, 8338–8341, 8882.

[30] Ferdinand A. Silcox, *Report of the Forester, 1936* (Washington: Government Printing Office, 1936), pp. 42–44; Nixon, *Roosevelt and Conservation*, II, 445–448, 493–494, 505, 535–538; *Congressional Record*, 74 Cong. 2 Sess., pp. 2895–2896, 2941–2944, 8338–8341, 8882.

Although congressional disapproval of funds for the shelter-belt work was disappointing to project officials, it did not halt their efforts to gain recognition for the undertaking. Secretary Henry Wallace proposed a plan for developing farm forestry for the entire nation, a scheme that would be inclusive enough to authorize the shelterbelt project. Wallace reasoned that "a flank attack . . . [would] make any opposition constitute in reality oposition [*sic*] to a national development of a farm forestry, a subject in which the majority of . . . Congress have a direct interest."[31] Wallace's idea won the President's approval and became the heart of a bill introduced by Senator Norris on May 30, 1936, which provided for federal assistance to farmers in the planting of windbreaks and woodland lots on the nation's farms. Representative Marvin Jones of Texas introduced a companion measure in the House a few days later. The Norris-Jones measure sought to cure the lack of authorization that stigmatized the shelterbelt affair. Again, Senator Norris's proposal won Senate approval, but House opposition let the bill die in committee.[32] Thus, when Congress adjourned in June, 1936, the shelterbelt project had neither been approved nor financed, and it faced liquidation.

While Congress debated the project's fate, the shelterbelt forces planted trees. The 1936 season witnessed the planting of ten times as many trees as that in the previous spring. More than 17,000,000 young trees were established during the second season. The tree strips measured 1,152 linear miles. The cost to the government was estimated at seven cents per tree. In preparation

[31] Nixon, *Roosevelt and Conservation*, I, 529.
[32] *Congressional Record*, 74 Cong. 2 Sess., pp. 8366, 8622, 9020, 9169, 9442.

for the future, the workers planted more than 50,000,000 seed-lings in the nurseries. These successes seemed to warrant that the project should be continued, but the shelterbelt authorities began to liquidate the venture as Congress had mandated.[33]

Finally, when all seemed hopeless, President Roosevelt and the WPA came to their rescue. An allotment of $1,200,000 was made available for the next fiscal season (July 1, 1936, to June 30, 1937). The congressional appropriation of $170,000 was not used and all liquidating activity ceased. At this time the Forest Service renamed the undertaking the "Prairie States Forestry Project." The decision to relabel the work appears to indicate that greater emphasis was needed on the relationship between the scheme and the WPA, its benefactor, since Congress had rejected the plains tree-growing as a major conservation program. Further, use of the new name may have represented an attempt to disassociate the project from the ridicule it had suffered in its earlier days.[34]

When the next fiscal year arrived, it apparently was deemed wise not to seek congressional authorization and financial support. The endeavor again was supplied funds from WPA appropriations. It was apparent, though, that congressional anger might be encountered if the project did not win approval. Thus, in 1937, Senator Norris once more put the Wallace strategy in the form of an authorization bill for the newly-named Prairie States Forestry Project. Once again the Nebraska Senator was successful in winning Senate approval. In the House, Representative Walter Doxey, a Mississippi Democrat, co-sponsored the

33 Perry, "Prairie States Forestry Project," p. 55; Silcox, *Report of the Forester*, 1936, p. 43.

34 Perry, "Prairie States Forestry Project," p. 55.

bill. The new measure, the Cooperative Farm Forestry Act, re-
sembled the previous bill, but it contained significant alterations.
The changes represented concessions to the opponents of the
shelterbelt. Specifically, the undertaking was no longer to be an
action program administered from Washington as it had been
from 1934 to 1937. Thereafter it would be a cooperative venture among the Forest Service, land-grant colleges, and state
forestry agencies. The cost of the undertaking would be shared
by the government and the farmer. Another change of note was
the prohibition in the bill that forbade the Forest Service to open
nurseries in competition with private nurserymen. The provisions
mollified powerful interests who opposed any venture that re-
channeled federal funds from their traditional course through
state agencies and then to the cultivator.[35]

The Norris-Doxey Act or the Cooperative Farm Forestry Act
became law on May 18, 1937. Although the shelterbelt project
was not mentioned in the bill, the terms of the law were broad
enough to include the planting of shelterbelts on the farms of the
plains farmer. Shelterbelt proponents now needed to gain financial backing from Congress. An immediate attempt was made to
obtain it. Officials of the Department of Agriculture sought to
obtain approval of an outright appropriation item for the venture in a deficiency appropriation bill that was under consideration by the House when the farm forestry bill was enacted. Congress again refused to appropriate on the grounds that no emergency existed where the plains tree-growing plan was concerned.
Failure to win financial support left the undertaking mainly a

[35] *The New York Times*, August 1, 4, 1936; Reisch, "FDR and Conservation," pp. 292–293; *Congressional Record*, 75 Cong. 1 Sess., pp.
3617–3624, 9446.

WPA project instead of an independent program with distinctive budgetary status.[36]

For the next three years the project officials were content to plant trees on a cooperative basis with the farmer. The funds for the affair were furnished by the WPA at presidential request. Approximately two and a quarter million dollars annually were supplied to the Department of Agriculture to cover planting costs. The money was made available under a provision in the WPA appropriation that permitted the use of federal funds for any federally-sponsored project. The financial tie between the Prairie States Forestry Project and the WPA was in general a happy one. However, it grew less cheerful as World War II neared.[37]

By 1940, the problem of funding the endeavor became so critical that Secretary Wallace advised the President that the project might have to be abandoned. He complained that WPA rules were so restrictive that many facets of the venture could not be carried on under such inflexible regulations. Ninety per cent of their funds had to be used for labor expenses, and the remaining ten per cent was not adequate to finance the supervisory, technical, and research operations of the undertaking. Further complication stemmed from the fact that the project utilized its labor on a seasonal basis.

Wallace appealed to the President to give the project distinctive budgetary status within the Emergency Relief Appropriation Act for fiscal year 1941. The President and the Budget Di-

36 Nixon, *Roosevelt and Conservation*, II, 445–449, 535–538; Perry, "Prairie States Forestry Project," pp. 55–56.

37 Perry, "Prairie States Forestry Project," pp. 56–59; Nixon, *Roosevelt and Conservation*, II, 439–441, 448–449.

rector doubted the wisdom of such a course in view of prior congressional actions and attitudes. The Secretary was advised to make plans to phase out the project and to transfer its activities to the Soil Conservation Service, which had been steadily organizing conservation districts in the prairie states. Interestingly, Congress appropriated $300,000 for farm forestry under the Norris-Doxey Act but specifically prohibited the use of these funds for the shelterbelt scheme. As usual, the project received a WPA allocation of some two million dollars for its use through June 30, 1941.[38]

Neither the Department of Agriculture nor the Forest Service made any effort to implement the President's suggestion to merge the shelterbelt project with the conservation activities of the Soil Conservation Service. Again in 1941, when budgets for 1942 and 1943 were being developed, the Department of Agriculture, then headed by Claude R. Wickard, sought distinctive status for the project but was unable to get presidential approval. Clearly, the Director of the Budget, Harold D. Smith, wisely saw that there was no need for both the Soil Conservation Service and the Prairie States Forestry Project to engage in duplication and overlapping of functions. At the height of these considerations, Senator Norris embarrassingly obtained the first direct appropriation for the project from Congress.[39] This windfall, along with a WPA allotment, once again enabled the project to preserve its independence for a time. Nevertheless, when budgets for fiscal year 1943 were in the planning stages the Budget Director in-

[38] *Ibid.*
[39] Perry, "Prairie States Forestry Project," pp. 69–70; Nixon, *Roosevelt and Conservation*, II, 535–538; *Congressional Record*, 75 Cong. 3 Sess., pp. 2988–2989, 77 Cong. 1 Sess., pp. A–5520–5522.

sisted that the project be transferred to the Soil Conservation Service.[40]

Uncertainty over future financing, resistance from the Budget Bureau, inattention from President Roosevelt, who was busy with foreign affairs, and the ever-widening program of the Soil Conservation Service in the plains states—all contributed to Secretary Wickard's decision on October 31, 1941, to transfer the Prairie States Forestry Project from the Forest Service to the Soil Conservation Service. Wickard's decision to effect the transfer and bring an end to the tree-planting venture as a separate project was probably a wise one, but it also was unwelcome to both the Forest Service and Senator Norris.[41] Both felt that tree planting under the Soil Conservation Service would suffer because other measures might be substituted for tree planting for erosion control. The President approved the transfer, and on July 1, 1942, the plains tree-planting scheme became a part of the larger New Deal effort to conserve the soils of the prairie states from wind and water erosion.[42]

During the eight-year life of the enterprise much was accomplished. Since the planting of the first belts in March, 1935, several investigations of the belts have been conducted. Determinations of the value of the belts to crops and cattle and of public attitudes toward the tree strips have been made. Particular attention has been given to the growth and survival rate of the trees and to the effectiveness of the belts in reducing wind velocity. A 1944 investigative team found that "in terms of meeting the

[40] Nixon, *Roosevelt and Conservation*, II, 535–538.

[41] Perry, "Prairie States Forestry Project," pp. 71–72; Nixon, *Roosevelt and Conservation*, II, 535–538.

[42] *Ibid.*

main purpose for which the belts were established, that of protection against wind, the Project was a success."[43] Survival rate
in 1944 for the area as a whole was 78 per cent. Growth of the
trees during their first ten years was described as striking. In
1944, benefits from the belts were already accruing, although the
belts were less than ten years old. Benefits listed included land-
scape improvement, control of wind erosion, cover for game
birds, the creation of snow traps along highways, and many
others.[44]

In the summer of 1954, Forest Service officials re-examined
the condition of the belts and reviewed the project's planting
program. This evaluation, made twenty years after the first trees
were planted, revealed that over 220,000,000 trees had been
planted on 30,000 farms, creating a total of 18,600 linear miles
of tree strips during the eight-year life of the shelterbelt program.
The latter study was more critical of the work of the project.
The reviewers found that the belts planted in the 1930's would
have been more efficient if the design of the windbreaks, the
species composition of the belts, and the spacing and arrangement of the trees within the belts had been changed. Other criticisms of the examiners included the charge that the early planters failed to adhere to the primary goal—that of planting to
produce effective wind barriers. Some belts were planted to obtain wood products or fruit and for esthetic results. It also was
pointed out that the early belts were too wide, lacked sufficient

[43] Munns and Stoeckeler, "How Are the Great Plains Shelterbelts?"
p. 57.
[44] *Ibid.*; Dahl, "Development of the Prairie States Forestry Project,"
pp. 301–306.

evergreen stock, and often were planted too close to roads. Farmers were criticized for allowing cattle to destroy the belts in portions of Texas and Oklahoma where open range existed. The trees continued to grow and the survival rate was judged to be 70 to 80 per cent in 1954.[45]

Undoubtedly, the shelterbelts are surviving and are very much in evidence from Texas to Canada. From 1934 to 1942, the Forest Service spent about $14,000,000 for the project. Were these funds wasted, as many charged they would be when the project was inaugurated? A 1961 study by the Forest Service reveals that substantial economic benefits have resulted. In North Dakota, windbreaks increase the corn yield by six bushels an acre. Cattle consume less feed when protected by windbreaks. More cotton is harvested from Texas and Oklahoma fields if shelterbelts line the field on the south and west.[46]

The real proof of the economic value of the shelterbelt is best evidenced by the willingness of the farmer to expend his own funds for tree planting. North Dakota farmers planted almost as many miles of tree strips in 1960 as were planted in any year by the Prairie States Forestry Project. President Roosevelt regarded the project as successful. Three days before his death on April 12, 1945, he sought information about the progress of the venture. His interests centered on the value of the belts to a com-

[45] Ralph A. Read, *The Great Plains Shelterbelt in 1954* (Publication No. 16 of the Great Plains Agricultural Council, Lincoln, Nebraska, 1958), pp. 8–10, 77–81, 87–90, 116–125.

[46] Arthur H. Carhart, "Shelterbelts," pp. 76–77; J. H. Stoeckeler, "Shelterbelt Influences on Great Plains Field Environment and Crops," Production Research Report No. 62 (USDA, Forest Service, 1962).

munity and to a typical plains family, and on their effectiveness in increasing crop yields.[47] It appears that the President may have had in mind the renewal of the project when World War II ended. Roosevelt never read the report, but each annual report of the Forest Service provides an answer. In 1965, approximately 40,458 acres of the plains were converted into forests in the form of tree belts.[48] The Forest Service once again has major responsibility for the venture. Thus, what began as an idea in the denuded hills of Montana became one of the most controversial forestry projects ever undertaken. What was once regarded as "one of the most ridiculous and silly proposals that was ever submitted to the American people"[49] in the course of the New Deal years became a whole new departure in forestry— plains forestry!

[47] Nixon, *Roosevelt and Conservation,* II, 643–644; National Archives, *Records of the National Planning Board: Selected Publications Relating to Forest Conservation, The Shelterbelt Program* (Washington, National Archives, Record Group 187), pp. 167–174.

[48] Edward P. Cliff, *Report of The Chief of the Forest Service, 1965* (Washington: Government Printing Office, 1966), p. 33.

[49] *Congressional Record,* 74 Cong. 2 Sess., p. 2942.

New Deal Critics: Did They Miss the Point?

BY GEORGE WOLFSKILL

HAROLD ICKES, the new Secretary of Interior, who had known all the ups and downs in the battle for reform, could be forgiven his enthusiasm in the first, frantic days of the New Deal. "By God," he declared, "I never thought I'd live to see this. Why, this is a second honeymoon."[1]

But the New Deal honeymoon of which Ickes spoke did not last, could not last. For many the romance faded, disenchantment set in, then estrangement, and, finally, total alienation. Why, one wonders, did Roosevelt and the New Deal, grappling as it were with "the trials of Job," inspire such distrust, such massive opposition in some quarters, such savage criticism? And was the distrust, the opposition, the criticism justified?

The starting point in the quest for answers would appear inevitable. It was the Depression: the shock, the despair, the disbelief that was a part of it. It was the Depression: the vulgar

---

[1] Quoted in Eric Goldman, *Rendezvous With Destiny* (New York: Alfred A. Knopf, 1956), p. 268.

enormity, the sinister insidiousness of it. The American people reacted to the Depression and the nature of that reaction was clearly reflected in the nation's response to the New Deal. In the national calamity Roosevelt was either friend or foe; the New Deal left few people neutral.

Most of the critics, it would seem, fell into well-defined categories. This is not to say that there were not some, perhaps many, who could not be easily catalogued: those who were critical of a particular program or policy, those who were unhappy because some special desire went unfulfilled, those who found unpalatable some personality in the Administration, even those who, for whatever reason, found Roosevelt personally offensive. But these were not the persistent denouncers and nay-sayers, nor were they the people who joined organizations, attended meetings, distributed literature, lent financial support, and in every other way possible sought to unhorse Franklin Roosevelt.

Among those who may be considered serious critics of the New Deal were three groups at one end of the political spectrum, the Communists, the Socialists, and (for lack of a better name) the Radicals. It is true that after 1935, when the international party line shifted to the Popular Front approach, American Communists suddenly became all sweetness and light, cleancut disciples of patriotic virtue. But this was only a matter of tactics. Roosevelt, they thought, was their best defense against home-grown fascism—at least for the time being. So they supported Roosevelt. Some even voted for him in 1936. But they despised Roosevelt, and in the early years of the New Deal they attacked him openly and relentlessly.

If the Communists despised Roosevelt, the Socialists and Radicals merely pitied him. To non-Communists on the political left

Roosevelt was a decent, well-meaning, though half-hearted liberal and the New Deal was a mass of halfway, piecemeal legislation offering a sedative of relief—not enough to do any real
good, just enough, they feared, to still the voices of political and
social protest. The Socialist leader, Norman Thomas, one of
Roosevelt's most vocal critics, about said it all when he accused
the New Deal of trying "to cure tuberculosis with cough drops."[2]

At the other end of the political spectrum were the native Fascists, dreaming their dreams of an America, Nazi-style. As late
as 1939, there were in the United States an estimated eight hundred organizations that could be called pro-Fascist. Some had the
word "Fascist" in their names. A few used the swastika, or
something approaching it, as part of their insignia. Most of them
had a lot to say about Jews, about ethnic minorities, about Communists and other favorite scapegoats. They talked of wondrous
things, of wanting to champion democracy and Christianity, to
protect individualism and free enterprise, and to save the country from something or other. Always on their lips was grave
concern for the Bible, for the faith of the fathers, for the Constitution, and for "the American way of life." All these things and
more. And they hated Franklin Roosevelt.

Strung out at intervals along the spectrum were other groups
of Roosevelt critics. They included a more than substantial part
of the American business community, the professions, the press,
and the Republican party, all rallying under the banner of what
is traditionally described as political conservatism. In the Congress this conservatism eventually assumed the form of a

[2] Norman Thomas, *Is the New Deal Socialist?* (New York: Socialist
Party of America, 1936), p. 5.

Republican-Southern Democratic coalition which, after 1937, fought Roosevelt to a standoff.

Criticism of Roosevelt by all of these opposition groups made sense, a great deal of sense, if one were willing to accept their premises. The Communists, who, until the party-line switch in 1935, called Roosevelt a social Fascist and the New Deal a dictatorship designed to gut the worker and betray the working masses, hated Roosevelt because they hated the system. Communists feared and despised a capitalist future which Roosevelt was trying to insure. Socialists and non-Communist Radicals were frustrated by dreams of what the future could be. Roosevelt was doing too little too slowly for too few, and he was trying to do it through a patched-up capitalist system. The golden opportunity, the opportunity to effect a Socialist revolution, they lamented, was slipping through his fingers like sand. The dreadful consequence of this lost opportunity would, they believed, be some form of fascism. The right-wing extremists, the native Fascist crowd, opposed Roosevelt for essentially the same reasons. They, too, were aiming for a new system. Despite their insistence that they sought only to save and preserve America from the ravages of the New Deal, their goal was revolution, a new order. And Roosevelt stood astride their path.

Business leaders sensed early that Roosevelt did not define "recovery" as they did, that he did not mean to re-establish the old order, did not intend to return business to the head of the line. Roosevelt, they felt, was making them the whipping boy of the Depression. Those who customarily saw things their way, the professional groups, the press, particularly the big-city press (itself a business and crucially dependent on advertising), the Republican party, and a large bloc in the Congress took up the refrain. Loud and long were the lamentations over broken promises, extravagant spending, experimentation, incipient socialism or worse, increased taxes, bureaucracy, regimentation, snooping, centralization, flaunting of the Constitution and states' rights, an endless list of New Deal sins, all of which added up to one thing: Roosevelt was going, had gone, too damn far. Recovery, so their argument ran, was already on the way before Roosevelt became President. Had he just let things alone, just let nature take its course, everything would have turned out all right. But his dangerous bungling was prolonging the Depression and might lead to something worse.

Nothing Roosevelt might have done would have satisfied his critics of the extreme left or extreme right short of abject surrender and a repudiation of everything the nation had held dear for nearly a century and a half—in short, a revolution. That was unthinkable and the thought never crossed Roosevelt's mind. No, there would be no seduction by Communist or Fascist flummery as had occurred in other countries.

But what, then? What of criticism by those whose sincere intentions were to conserve, protect, and restore? Men who likewise gave no thought to changing the basic system? Wise men, men whose motives were above reproach, men who looked Roosevelt in the eye and insisted he was wrong, dead wrong? In the last analysis, these were the critics who mattered.

Much, if not most, of the trouble was from misunderstanding, from failing to interpret what the New Deal was and what Roosevelt was trying to do. For one thing, critics could not identify the New Deal in terms of philosophy or ideology. There seemed no evidence of a coherent and consistent set of principles from which Roosevelt was operating. There was considerable truth in this charge. Roosevelt continually sought to disengage himself from ideological commitments. Consistent the New Deal was not. Critics could complain that Roosevelt was pragmatic, eclectic, experimental, anything that suggested trial and error, and they would be correct. As Hugh Johnson, deposed head of the National Recovery Administration, put it in 1937, Roosevelt would go down in history as "the man who started more creations than were ever begun since Genesis—and finished none."[3] Johnson did not mean that, of course; but it was an interesting way of saying that Roosevelt was at least willing to undertake the new and untried, which usually implied that he did not know what he was doing.

Yet here was another point at which critics misunderstood the New Deal. The New Deal was not aimless experimentation. Innovation, yes. A willingness to defy convention, yes. But this spirit of the New Deal did not mean that it had no sense of direction, no ultimate destination. After Roosevelt had been a year and four months in office, the *New Republic*, in an article entitled "The Show is Over," described the disillusionment and discouragement of his more radical supporters in the administration, men who despaired of the New Deal, men who lamented over his failure to aim for complete nationalization at a dead run.[4] The talk by Rexford Tugwell and others about rolling up their sleeves and making the country over was only talk. They would never get the chance. The evidence was already mounting

[3] Radio address by Hugh Johnson, June 15, 1937, quoted in Congressional Record, 75th Congress, 1st Session (1937), p. 1708.

[4] Jonathan Mitchell, "The Show Is Over," *New Republic* (July 25, 1934), pp. 282–284.

that Roosevelt and his New Deal were neither communistic nor socialistic, not even radical enough to suit the radicals.

The absence of ideological content and the pragmatic innovations likewise contradicted another common criticism, that the New Deal was some brand of alien crusade. The New Deal was, indeed, a call to arms, and it was built on faith—both characteristics of crusades. But faith in the New Deal was not for some far-off better tomorrow but a better today. And the call to arms was for action now, a pragmatic attack on national problems as they were, not as they may have been preconceived by crusading prophets of reform. And when critics insisted the New Deal was a revolution, they were wrong if they meant anything resembling the ideological upheavals shaking Europe. From first to last the New Deal was put to the acid test, the test of the ballot box. And the hand-to-hand combat between rival parties for public support went on as before. The legislative branch could frustrate Roosevelt, and did. And, like all presidents before him, Roosevelt held his breath, crossed his fingers, and hoped for the best when his programs were challenged in the courts. No, the New Deal was neither crusade nor revolution.

Critics were led into misunderstanding the New Deal for other reasons, too. They paid far too much attention to Roosevelt the man, the symbol of the New Deal. They spent too much time wringing their hands over New Deal personnel, over the Brain Trust and the people around Roosevelt. They were misled by New Deal techniques, particularly the reliance on emergency, the mood of urgency which thrived on "must" legislation and what critics called "crisis" government. They spent too much energy trying to fathom the New Deal by analyzing specific poli-

cies and pieces of legislation. Some were thrown off the scent by
Roosevelt's apparent lack of reverence for states' rights and the
Constitution. Others were dismayed by Roosevelt's apolitical attitude, his obvious lack of confidence in political parties, and the
conspicuous decline in importance of traditional Democratic
party leaders.

But the New Deal could not rest its case on whether people
liked Franklin Roosevelt. The New Deal could not stand or fall
on the quality and caliber of men responsible for carrying it into
execution, or be judged solely on the basis of specific acts or
even specific mistakes. The New Deal had to be weighed in larger scales, against a larger background. Decisions had to be
reached regarding the whole New Deal, its aims and accomplishments, and the motivation of both. The crucial question remained. And the answer to that question baffled and eluded New
Deal critics. The question was: What was the New Deal?

Loud claims that the New Deal was "fascism" or "commu-
nism" or some other dangerous "ism" were tossed around indis-
criminately during the 1930's. They represented a state of mind
of many people, an unreasoning fear that any departure from the
status quo, however tentative, was a giant stride toward some
dreadful, confusing fate. Such charges could not be ignored.
They were to be taken seriously, but not too literally. The New
Deal was not fascism; Fascists said it was not. It was not com-
munism: Communists said it was not. That the New Deal was
assailed from both extremes is one fair sign that Roosevelt stood
somewhere in the shifting political center.

But if Roosevelt's goals for the New Deal were not communistic or fascistic, neither were they designed to lead the country
back to some imaginary golden age, an age of ancient virtues,

political quietism, and McKinley-like piety. Few would admit that the system worked none too well even then for the great majority of the American people. Yet so many of the New Deal critics, especially leaders of American business and industry and finance in the 1930's, had begun their climb to wealth and power, and sometimes fame, in the late nineteenth century that Social Darwinism was bred in their bones. Their political vision was clouded by nostalgia for what they regarded as the good old days, the American way of life, the system that had made America great. Roosevelt, to use his own words, had long since made it clear that he did not intend "to restore that ancient order."[5]

One way to describe the New Deal might be to say that it was an attempt to democratize industrial and finance capitalism, to see to it that its fruits were more fairly distributed, that its knavery was permanently curbed. It was, as Herbert Agar put it, a program to promote wide-spread prosperity without "the obscenities of Big Business."[6] Moderate as those objectives may have been, they nonetheless involved Roosevelt in one of the great issues of American political history. Broadly speaking, American presidents have been of two types. The one conceived of a federal government with limited powers, viewed national government with suspicion, and considered the office of Chief Executive to be exclusively administrative. The other accepted an ever-expanding role for federal government, particularly for the executive branch, as problems multiplied and as life in an industrialized society became increasingly complex.

[5] George Wolfskill, *The Revolt of the Conservatives* (Boston: Houghton Mifflin Company, 1962), p. 19.

[6] Herbert Agar, "The Task for Conservation," *American Review* (April, 1934), p. 10.

The contrast was plainly evident in the case of Roosevelt and his predecessor, Hoover. To say, or even to imply, that Hoover did nothing to check the Depression is grossly unfair. But it is true that in his approach there was a strong tendency to let nature take its course, a tendency to distrust governmental power, and a reluctance to extend federal authority.

Such reticence was manifestly not the case with Franklin Roosevelt. On the contrary, Roosevelt regarded government, federal government, the great healer and the Chief Executive the confident physician applying its curative powers. In this sense the New Deal meant an acceleration of and the stretching of federal powers, a steady concentration of authority in Washington with an equally steady decline of states' powers and individual rights, an expanding bureaucracy, an increasing emphasis on planning, and the inevitable charge that these things led the way to autocracy and dictatorship. In the minds of many no objective, however commendable, justified the use of such means; in fact, the use of such means would, they believed, inevitably defeat the objective.

Still another way to define the New Deal is to say that Roosevelt and the New Dealers rejected the concept that America was a finished product. With some critics this led to the sincere conviction that the New Deal was a break with tradition. Theirs was the concept of history as having run its course; the historical process was as finished and complete as the Great Pyramid. The American Revolution was the mighty groan of a people straining every muscle, every nerve, to shove the apex stone in place. And now it was finished, at last things were as they should be, a handsome thing to be admired and revered through the ages, its excesses and stupidities buried deep inside with the mummified pharaoh.

But the New Deal was, if nothing else, committed to the fact of constant, steady change, the necessity for governmental action to accommodate to those changes, and the continuing need for explaining to the people, in simple, candid terms, what those changes were all about. There was, then, a strong element of relativity about the New Deal, the belief that democracy was a method, a process, that was ever in a state of becoming, not a fulfilled system of economics, or government, or society, reduced to commandments and preserved on stones, writ by the finger of God.

Roosevelt and the New Deal applied to the Constitution something of that same spirit of change, of relativity, of dynamism. It was not that Roosevelt was flagrantly unconcerned about the supreme law of the land, that he rejected constitutional methods, that he deliberately sought to flout the Constitution, circumvent it, and, when the moon was right, murder it. He recognized, however, that it was capable of many interpretations (at least it always had been in the past). And he did not intend to stand idly by if it meant letting people starve by strict constitutional methods. If honest men who stood in awe of the Bible could differ, sometimes vehemently, over its meaning, so other men equally honest could dispute the meanings of the Constitution, which, after all, was not Holy Writ. John Franklin Carter, the Unofficial Observer of the New Deal years, was fairly close to the New Deal position when, in his customary humorous forthrightness, he wrote: "The New Dealers have no designs against the Constitution, provided that it retains the elasticity of the original fabric. This elasticity has always been in evidence whenever a Philadelphia lawyer desired to drive a corporate caravan through it, but it has been remarkably rigid whenever the rights of the common men were up for consideration."[7]

Just as the New Deal was committed to change, so was it committed to the proposition that governmental power was not automatically evil. Power and evil were not the same thing; power could be used for good as readily as for evil; power could only be judged in its specific applications. What the New Dealers were getting at was that there could never be in modern society a moratorium on the use of power. Power existed, it was; if it were not held in one place it would be held in another. There could not be a power vacuum. If government refused to exercise its power, particularly in economic matters, there were those who would exercise it privately, as New Dealers believed had been the case for years. They believed, sincerely and conscientiously, that the default by government in its use of power had produced an economic situation grossly unfair, one in which the great rank and file of the American people consistently got the short end of the stick.

For the criticisms that the New Deal was a power-grabbing, tradition-shattering philosophy, dedicated to change just for the sake of change, the New Dealers themselves had to share much of the blame. They invited such an image of the New Deal, albeit for different reasons. The image they sought to create was one of boldness, daring, courage, imagination, a willingness to experiment, to try the untried, to launch out on uncharted seas. In this they probably went too far. And in singing the praises of

---

[7] Unofficial Observer, *The New Dealers* (New York: Simon and Schuster, 1934), p. 392.

Roosevelt they unwittingly created the image of a leader that was indeed too good to be true, of a leader such as had not been seen in the land since Isaiah.

Some critics took a long, hard look at the New Deal and mistakenly decided it was an attempt to destroy business, to unhinge the capitalist system. Despite what often looked like a vendetta with business, industrial capitalism and the free enterprise system were never really in any danger from the New Deal. From the first, Roosevelt expected to save the system, to cure its malaise. But he did not intend to do so because private business was somehow sacred. His was a pragmatic choice, not a theological one; a choice based on experience, not a divine admonition that had been handed down from on high on a pillar of fire. A system of private business, if it were conducted properly, was the best system in America to serve the public interest. Roosevelt was convinced of that. But business could no longer do as it pleased and call it free enterprise.

New Deal convictions about business and the economic policies undertaken were based on a number of serious assumptions. Roosevelt, early in the game, discarded the proposition that the economy moved in mysterious cycles of boom and bust, governed by immutable laws that mere mortals could not comprehend. "No government," Hoover had declared categorically in 1936, "can legislate away the morning after any more than it can legislate away the effects of a tornado—not even the New Deal."[8] The "morning after" of which Hoover spoke was the inevitable hangover from a prosperity spree, as inevitable and irresistible as a tornado.

[8] Herbert Hoover, *American Ideals Versus the New Deal* (New York: E. Richard, 1936), p. 77.

Roosevelt refused to accept the assumption—and the spirit of resignation to a blind destiny implied in it—that the economic system was some whimsical, capricious, unpredictable thing that could bring pleasure or pain as it wished, and that there was nothing anybody could do about it. The conflict here was between those who believed that operation of the economic system had to be automatic, that it was some kind of perpetual motion machine, and those who put their trust in legislation to regulate and to assist the functioning of the system.

This New Deal commitment led to the conclusion that by wise planning and precautions prosperity was a happy state that could be created and depression avoided. Planning, as in the case of the National Industrial Recovery Act and the Agricultural Adjustment Act, was one of the prime excuses for charges of dictatorship, of conflicting claims of fascism and socialism leveled at the New Deal. As an aside, it did little good to point out to critics that at the outset, businessmen and farm leaders had favored such planning, that the NIRA and AAA were largely designed, not by New Dealers, but by businessmen and farmers to save themselves.

There was at least one other reason for the New Deal's appearing to be anti-business. That was the assumption (a mistaken assumption, as everyone eventually realized) that the United States had reached its maximum economic growth—the mature economy principle, it was called. The ability of the country to produce had far outstripped the capacity of the country to consume. If prosperity were to be restored, production and consumption must be restored to some sort of equilibrium.

The alternatives were to stimulate consumption, reduce production, or try some combination of both. The New Deal did all of these, but the emphasis was on limiting production. Some New Deal measures, such as plowing under cotton and slaughtering pigs, made little sense except in this context. But in any case, if the road to prosperity was through limited production and artificial scarcity, a large degree of government planning and government regulation was inevitable.

The attempt to restore economic balance and to reconcile individual freedom with twentieth-century industrialization invited, perhaps required, an emphasis on regulation and planning and on social welfare and security for the individual citizen. But none of this meant that business, or capitalism, or free enterprise had much of anything to fear from the New Deal. There might be grounds for serious discussion of which political party and which group might best implement the techniques. But the Depression had hastened the day and had forced upon the country acceptance of the proposition that, like it or not, government was destined to play an ever-expanding role in the daily life, particularly the economic life, of the country. Only the politically ossified insisted it was not true.

The New Deal acted on this assumption. Roosevelt, despite charges of being a traitor to his class, undertook to apply it without disturbing the foundations of the existing system. The NRA fostered monopoly and combatted the dangerously deflationary effect of ruthless price-cutting. His programs against parasitic holding companies, stock market riggers, dishonest bankers, and irresponsible employers were attempts to save the system from the vulgar avarice of some of its practitioners, to save it from perhaps even more extreme solutions. Mortgage relief, subsidy

payments, minimum wages, ready credit, work relief, public
works, and the like were designed to bolster the system as well as
to provide security and a helping hand to the underdog.

For those who would be critics of Roosevelt and the New Deal
there was something for everybody. Men found ample excuse
(and sometimes just cause) for criticizing Roosevelt personally,
for criticizing at least some of the people around him, for criticizing specific New Deal policies, techniques, attitudes. Any or
all of these forms of criticism were to be expected; they happened to one degree or another in every administration.

The unpleasant fact, the deplorable fact, was that massive opposition mounted on so many fronts was the principal obstacle
that prevented Roosevelt from achieving the ultimate goals of
the New Deal. Roosevelt was never able to make clear to the
American people where the New Deal was going, what it really
meant to do; and men, unfortunately, were not able to fathom
it merely by watching the New Deal in action. There was from
first to last appalling misunderstanding about the philosophy of
the New Deal.

It is true, of course, that most Americans understood and prof-
ited by some of the objectives of the New Deal. America was
all the better for a social and ethnic revolution which for the first
time revised upward the status of great groups of the "forgotten
men" in American society, provided them with unprecedented
opportunity for escaping a dull and humdrum existence, offered
them fulfillment. America was a better place because Roosevelt
succeeded in making security for the individual something more
than an idle wish; it became an attainable dream, and an accept-
able part of American political philosophy. America was better off
because the New Deal had championed the right of others be-

sides businessmen to participate in decision-making, particularly those decisions affecting economic policy.

And there were signs, heartening signs, that the country was at long last coming of age, arriving, finally, at a stage of maturity when problems, any problems, could be solved by politics rather than by inflexible ideology or, worse, by violence. This may be the principal explanation of why the New Deal was so incomprehensible to that considerable host of New Deal critics who kept thrusting forward their preconceived solutions to the nation's ills. The New Deal was, as one writer has put it, "not a 'scheme' but a 'deal' so different from the political solitaire which the ideologue likes to play."[9]

And there were also clear signs that things would never again be as they once were. Roosevelt had succeeded in nationalizing politics, in concentrating and focusing attention on national government. Ever after, when men spoke of "the government" there was never any doubt but that they meant Washington. Washington, moreover, had become the capital of the nation in more than just a geographical sense, or even a political sense. It was now, for good or ill, the financial capital as well.

All of these things, and more, knowledgeable people could see and understand. And yet most Americans, I fear, friends or foes of Roosevelt, missed the real point of the New Deal. Certainly the critics did. Roosevelt refused to accept the narrow economic determinism implied in both socialism (whether it be of the Marxist variety or whatever) and laissez faire with its mystical faith in immutable economic laws. Roosevelt rejected the economic fatalism of the arrogant rugged individualist and the doc-

[9] Heinz Eulau, "Neither Ideology Nor Utopia: The New Deal in Retrospect," *Antioch Review* (Winter, 1959–1960), p. 536.

trinaire collectivist. He was convinced that there must be some
other way, a middle way. A modified capitalism, a mixed economy was possible, he believed. And he caught hell from all sides
for believing it. But once convinced that he was right, that there
was a middle way, Roosevelt burned bridges all over the place.
What began to emerge from the New Deal was a society that
had divorced itself from laissez faire but that refused to marry
socialism. But this was as far as Roosevelt got. He was never
able to apply the philosophy of the middle way to anything more
than the symptoms of the Depression. The crucial problems of
the twentieth century, the problems that had caused the disaster
in the first place, were not confronted; they remained unsolved.

The most serious problem confronting the country, challeng-
ing the minds of statesmen and theoreticians alike, straining the
fabric of the Constitution and the federal system to the breaking
point, was how to reconcile traditional freedom for the individual (the freedom of an individual in an agrarian society which
the country had inherited from the nineteenth century) with the
challenge of industrialization, centralization, monopoly, the mal-
distribution of wealth, urbanization, science and automation and
technology, all of those things which threatened, which undermined the American dream, which challenged Herbert Croly's
promise of American life. The individual versus the Industrial
Revolution was the unseen fear, sensed but uncomprehended,
felt but misunderstood by the Populists; it was uppermost in the
minds of every small-town Progressive businessman hunched
over his accounts and ledgers; it was the nagging imperative
which had commanded the attention of Theodore Roosevelt and
Woodrow Wilson, had provided a cause for the Muckrakers,
had produced the New Nationalism and the New Freedom. It

was the one important reality that escaped Herbert Hoover, that was overlooked in the sentimentalities of Henry Ford and the vulgar, almost sacrilegious irrelevancies of Bruce Barton.

The individual versus the Industrial Revolution was the prime domestic question of the twentieth century, and Roosevelt faced it in a time of economic disaster when the country was in no mood to listen to solutions that might right the country in some indefinite long run. People wanted action, they wanted it quick, and they wanted results. There was no time for seeking a middle way by careful probing, by judicious weighing, by intelligent and selective trial and error. The critics did not believe there was a middle way. It was the crowning irony of New Deal criticism that the classical liberal and the Marxist could meet on common ground and solemnly agree that the middle way was impossible, suicidally impossible; for both, the middle way consigned America to a life of economic sin or worse. The pressure for quick results and the dead weight of all-or-nothing, either-or obstructionism meant the New Deal could never be much more than a grand postponement. Roosevelt could be no more than a Fabius Maximus, the Dutch boy with his finger in the democratic dike.

The night of Roosevelt's death, Samuel Grafton, the syndicated columnist of the New York *Post*, did an obituary. Grafton may have had deeper insight into the New Deal dilemma than any critic or apologist, then or later, when he wrote:

> Leaf-raking was silly. You cannot tell me he did not know it was silly. He knew. But as against a concentration camp, it was noble. As against what happened in Spain, leaf-raking even had grandeur. I think he knew these things, and there was a knowledge of them in his smile when he was attacked and baited.
>
> He had no answers that were good for a hundred years. But in

> a six-month crisis he always had a six-month answer. . . . Maybe
> he had a right to smile, and to think that a billion was not so
> much; maybe he knew what he had got for it, and that it was
> a bargain.[10]

Under the circumstances a six-month answer for a six-month
crisis would have to do. Stall for time. Trade dollars for time.
Time. Time for the country to collect its wits. Time for the people to pull themselves together, shake their fears, recover their
sense of humor, take heart. Time so that America would not default to madmen and lunatics and their wicked schemes. Time
so that honest men could find solid answers to pressing problems
that the country had been ignoring and fending off for years.
Time to vindicate Roosevelt's dream of the middle way. He had
seen America through a great agony. Democracy had survived
its severest test; it was to have a second chance. As Grafton said,
the New Deal was a bargain; Roosevelt did have a right to smile.
The New Deal postponement had saved America for the time
being; but it would be up to other men to demonstrate that it
was worth saving.

[10] Quoted in Bernard Asbell, *When F.D.R. Died* (New York: Holt,
Rinehart and Winston, Inc., 1961), p. 113.

Franklin D. Roosevelt's
Supreme Court "Packing" Plan

BY WILLIAM E. LEUCHTENBURG

FRANKLIN D. ROOSEVELT'S PROPOSAL to "pack" the Supreme Court in 1937 bore the mark of a proud sovereign who after suffering many provocations had just received a new confirmation of his power. In November, 1936, the President had won the greatest electoral victory in the history of the two-party system. He had captured forty-six of the country's forty-eight states —all but Maine and Vermont—precisely as his campaign manager, James A. Farley, had predicted. Roosevelt was jubilant at the result. "I knew I should have gone to Maine and Vermont," he said, "but Jim wouldn't let me."[1]

Yet Roosevelt's sense of triumph was flawed by the realization that it was incomplete, for if he controlled the Executive office and could expect to have his way with Congress, where he had led his party to a smashing victory, the third branch, the Supreme Court, seemed intractable. Four of the justices—James McRey-

---

[1] Walter Johnson, *1600 Pennsylvania Avenue* (Boston, 1960), p. 90.

nolds, Pierce Butler, Willis Van Devanter, and George Suther-
land—were such staunch conservatives that almost every time
Roosevelt's Attorney General, Homer Cummings, went into
court, he knew he had four votes against him; if he lost even one
of the remaining five he would be beaten. Three judges—Louis
Brandeis, Harlan Fiske Stone, and Benjamin Cardozo—would
approve most of the New Deal laws. But if either of the two
justices in the center—Chief Justice Charles Evans Hughes or
Owen Roberts—joined the conservative "Four Horsemen,"
Roosevelt's program might perish in the courtroom.

Early in the New Deal, except for a relatively minor ruling
in the "hot oil" opinion,[2] the Supreme Court had appeared willing to uphold novel legislation. In two state cases and in the
"gold clause cases," the Court sustained emergency acts, although
each time by an uncomfortably close 5–4 margin.[3]

But in the spring of 1935 the roof fell in. Justice Roberts
joined the conservative four to invalidate a rail pension law,[4]
and thereafter Roberts voted with the conservatives on a number
of crucial cases. Later that same month, on Black Monday, May
27, 1935, the Court, this time in a unanimous decision, demol-
ished the National Industrial Recovery Act.[5] In the next year the

[2] Panama Refining Co. v. Ryan, 293 U.S. 388 (1935).

[3] Home Building & Loan Association v. Blaisdell et al., 290 U.S. 426
(1934); Nebbia v. New York, 291 U.S. 523 (1934); Perry v. United
States, 294 U.S. 330 (1935), and related cases.

[4] R.R. Retirement Board v. Alton R.R. Co., 295 U.S. 330 (1935).

[5] A.L.A. Schechter Poultry Corp. et al. v. United States, 295 U.S. 553
(1935). That same day, the Court dealt a personal blow to the President
in Humphrey's Executor v. U.S., 295 U.S. 602 (1935). William E.
Leuchtenburg, "The Case of the Contentious Commissioner: Humphrey's

Court, in a 6–3 decision, struck down the Agricultural Adjustment Act in an opinion by Justice Roberts that provoked a blistering dissent by Justice Stone; took special pains to knock out the Guffey Coal Act in the *Carter* case; and in the *Tipaldo* case invalidated a New York State minimum wage law.[6] Of all the wounds the Court inflicted on itself, the *Tipaldo* decision cut deepest. It appeared to create, as Roosevelt said, a "no-man's-land," in which neither the federal nor state governments could act to protect the worker.[7] At the end of the historic session, Justice Stone wrote: "We finished the term of Court yesterday, I think in many ways one of the most disastrous in its history."[8]

As Roosevelt contemplated his second term, a confrontation with the Supreme Court seemed inevitable. No doubt he wished to rebuke the justices for invalidating so much of the legislation passed in his first term, including the two big acts, the NIRA and the AAA. Even more important, the reasoning in such cases suggested that the Court would find still other laws unconstitutional when tests of these statutes reached it. In jeopardy in the next few months would be such landmarks as the Social Security Act and the Wagner National Labor Relations Act. But this was not all. Despite having won an unprecedented mandate, the Pres-

---

Executor *v.* U.S.," in Harold M. Hyman and Leonard W. Levy (eds.), *Freedom and Reform* (New York, 1967), pp. 276–312.

[6] United States *v.* Butler *et al.,* 297 U.S. 61 (1936); Carter *v.* Carter Coal Company, 298 U.S. 238 (1936); Morehead *v.* New York *ex rel.* Tipaldo, 298 U.S. 587 (1936).

[7] Samuel Rosenman (ed.), *The Public Papers and Addresses of Franklin D. Roosevelt* (13 vols., New York, 1938–1950), V, 191–192.

[8] Alpheus Thomas Mason, *Harlan Fiske Stone* (New York, 1956), p. 425.

ident felt constrained in asking Congress for new legislation, such as a wages and hours bill, because the Court might very well strike down these new measures too.

Was there a way out of the President's dilemma short of a direct confrontation? The most obvious course would be for Roosevelt to wait until one or more justices resigned or died, but he could not foresee how long a period this would be. Not a single justice had left the bench in his entire first term. No president since Andrew Johnson had served a full term without being able to appoint at least one new member of the Court. Many New Dealers thought—perhaps with reason—that some aged justices would, in other circumstances, have retired, but were deliberately remaining on the bench to frustrate the President. Some believed that some justices were deliberately staying alive in order to thwart him.

Possibly, too, the President might have waited to see whether the election returns had helped to change the minds of the justices. But this seemed a poor risk, given the record of the Court as recently as the previous spring. Moreover, many of the New Dealers sensed a special urgency. They perceived the crisis of the depression as a priceless opportunity to advance social legislation and wished to exploit the President's stunning victory, which gave new momentum to the drive for reform. If Roosevelt hesitated, the sense of crisis might diminish and the momentum would be lost.

Given Roosevelt's determination to reform the Judiciary, what method was he to choose?[9] He had many choices before him,

[9] The prelude to the 1937 fight is discussed at length in William E. Leuchtenburg, "The Origins of Franklin D. Roosevelt's 'Court-Packing'

most of them embracing some kind of constitutional amendment. Some proposed that the Court be limited to invalidating statutes only if it had a majority greater than 5–4. Others wanted to give Congress the right to re-enact laws by a two-thirds vote over an adverse decision. Still others wished to specify that Congress had broad authority to regulate labor conditions.

But these proposed constitutional amendments, it was argued, did not meet the problem posed by the Court's intransigence, or, if they did, they were not feasible politically. Roosevelt maintained that a constitutional amendment could not be ratified by a sufficient number of states, not at least in a reasonable period of time. "If you were not as scrupulous and ethical as you happen to be," he later wrote a prominent New York attorney who favored the amendment process, "you could make five million dollars as easy as rolling off a log by undertaking a campaign to prevent the ratification by one house of the Legislature, or even the summoning of a constitutional convention in thirteen states for the next four years. Easy money."[10]

Moreover, any legislation passed under the authorization of an amendment expanding the power of Congress would still be subject to review by the courts. "In view of what Mr. Justice Roberts did to a clause as broad and sweeping as 'the general welfare,'" observed the historian Charles Beard, "I can see other justices of his mental outlook macerating almost any clarifying

---

Plan," in Philip B. Kurland (ed.), *The Supreme Court Review* (Chicago, 1966), pp. 347–400.

10 Franklin D. Roosevelt to Charles C. Burlingham, Feb. 23, 1937, Franklin D. Roosevelt Library, Hyde Park, N.Y. (henceforth FDRL), PSF Supreme Court.

amendment less generous in its terms. If there is any phrase wider than providing for the general welfare, I am unable to conjure it up in my mind."[11]

Roosevelt reasoned that it was not the Constitution that needed to be changed but the Court. Increasingly, he turned to the idea of reform by an act of Congress rather than by amendment and to basing the law on a court-packing procedure founded on the principle of the age of the justices. In coming to this decision, he was influenced by the British precedent earlier in the century in the threat to pack the House of Lords. The specific device which Roosevelt and Cummings hit upon was one originally proposed for lower court justices by none other than Justice McReynolds when he had been Attorney General, and the President took a keen pleasure in that fact. But Roosevelt, who delighted in dramatic surprises, kept his decision a closely-guarded secret, hidden not only from his congressional leaders but even from his Cabinet and some of his intimates.

After the election, the President went off on a cruise to South America, while the country waited in expectation to see what legislation he would recommend for his second term. In January, Roosevelt gave his inaugural address without indicating what he planned to do. The new Congress convened, and more days passed, and still he did not let on what he was going to say. Then, abruptly, without warning, the President, on February 5, 1937, dropped a bombshell. Instead of calling for new social reforms, Roosevelt caught the nation, his congressional leaders, and his

[11] Charles A. Beard, "Rendezvous with the Supreme Court," *New Republic,* LXXX (Sept. 2, 1936), 93; Beard to Nicholas Kelley, Aug. 8, 1936, Mary Dewson MSS, FDRL, Box 6.

closest friends by surprise with a bold, quite unexpected proposal—to add six justices to the United States Supreme Court.

Roosevelt sent his scheme for reorganizing the Judiciary up to the Hill in a special message. The President claimed that insufficient personnel had resulted in overcrowded federal court dockets and had occasioned great delay and expense to litigants. "A part of the problem of obtaining a sufficient number of judges to dispose of cases is the capacity of the judges themselves," the President stated. "This brings forward the question of aged or infirm judges—a subject of delicacy and yet one which requires frank discussion."

"In exceptional cases, of course," Roosevelt conceded, "judges, like other men, retain to an advanced age full mental and physical vigor. Those not so fortunate are often unable to perceive their own infirmities. . . .

"A lower mental or physical vigor leads men to avoid an examination of complicated and changed conditions. Little by little, new facts become blurred through old glasses fitted, as it were, for the needs of another generation; older men, assuming that the scene is the same as it was in the past, cease to explore or inquire into the present or the future." Life tenure for judges, the President declared, "was not intended to create a static judiciary. A constant and systematic addition of younger blood will vitalize the courts. . . ."

To achieve this end, the President recommended that when a federal judge who had served at least ten years waited more than six months after his seventieth birthday to resign or retire, the President might add a new judge to the bench. He would appoint as many as, but not more than, six new justices to the

Supreme Court and forty-four new judges to the lower federal tribunals.[12] Since it seemed improbable that the justices would choose to resign, the plan was perceived to be an attempt to enlarge the Court.

The President's message generated an intensity of response unmatched by any legislative controversy of this century, save perhaps for the League of Nations episode. "No issue since the Civil War has so deeply split families, friends, and fellow lawyers," wrote one columnist.[13] Day after day, for the next half year, stories about the Supreme Court conflict rated banner headlines in the nation's press. One diarist noted: "Roosevelt's alteration plan of Supreme Court stirs America. Addresses, talks, arguments for and against it, everywhere."[14] The question was debated at town meetings in New England, at crossroads country stores in North Carolina, at a large rally at the Tulsa court house, by the Chatterbox Club of Rochester, New York, the Thursday Study Club of La Crosse, Wisconsin, the Veteran Fire Fighter's Association of New Orleans, and the Baptist Young People's Union of Lime Rock, Rhode Island.[15] In Beaumont, Texas, a

[12] *Public Papers of Franklin D. Roosevelt*, VI, 51–66. The Court bill also called for a number of procedural reforms.

[13] Paul Mallon, "Purely Confidential," Detroit *News*, Mar. 17, 1937.

[14] Margaret Fowler Dunaway MS Diary, Early March, 1937, Schlesinger Library, Radcliffe College, Cambridge, Mass. See also notes for a speech, Dorothy Kirchwey Brown MSS, Folder 14, Schlesinger Library.

[15] A. Roy Moore to John H. Kerr, Feb. 27, 1937, Kerr MSS, Southern Historical Collection, University of North Carolina, Chapel Hill, N.C., Box 9; S. R. Lewis to FDR, Feb. 19, 1937, National Archives, Dept. of Justice 235868; Rochester *Times Union*, Feb. 13, 1937, clipping, Frank Gannett MSS, Cornell University Collection of Regional History, Ithaca, N.Y., Box 2A; Mrs. C. I. Anderson to Merlin Hull, Feb. 19, 1937, Hull MSS, State Historical Society of Wisconsin, Madison, Wisc., Box 89;

movie audience broke out in applause for rival arguments on the Court plan when they were shown on the screen.[16]

Congressmen were inundated with communications from constituents on the Court bill. Senator Hiram Johnson of California reported: "I receive some hundreds of letters a day, all on the Court,—sometimes some thousands."[17] Senator Charles O. Andrews of Florida acknowledged: "We are receiving hundreds of letters regarding the Supreme Court and they have not been answered because it has been impossible to even read one-third, much less answer them. We have, however, answered many by working nights and Sundays."[18] Snowed under by 30,000 letters and telegrams, Senator Royal Copeland of New York said his office was "quite disorganized," and he pleaded for "some relief." "I feel fully informed of the wishes of my constituents," he added drily.[19]

No sooner was the message read in the House than the San Antonio congressman Maury Maverick raced down the aisle and dropped the bill in the hopper. But the Administration decided

---

W. C. Cray to John H. Overton, Mar. 21, 1937, Overton MSS, Dept. of Archives and Manuscripts, Louisiana State University, Baton Rouge, La., Box 2; June Beliveau to Theodore Green, Apr. 30, 1937, Green MSS, Library of Congress, Washington, D.C. (henceforth LC), Box 33.

[16] Beaumont *Enterprise*, Feb. 16, 1937, clipping, Arthur Vandenberg Scrapbooks, Michigan Historical Collections of The University of Michigan, Ann Arbor, Mich.

[17] Johnson to John Francis Neylan, Mar. 21, 1937, Johnson MSS, Bancroft Library, University of California, Berkeley, Calif.

[18] Charles O. Andrews to Charles Andrews, Jr., Mar. 2, 1937, Andrews MSS, P. K. Yonge Library of Florida History, University of Florida Libraries, Gainesville, Fla., Box 51.

[19] *Knickerbocker News*, Feb. 20, 1937, clipping, Royal Copeland Scrapbooks, Michigan Historical Collections.

to concentrate not on the House but on the Senate, in part because it wished to avoid a clash with another Texan, Hatton Sumners, the hostile chairman of the House Judiciary Committee, and with Speaker William Bankhead of Alabama, who resented Roosevelt's failure to take congressional leaders into his confidence.[20] However, even opponents of the plan conceded that the bill would be approved in the House with many votes to spare.[21]

The situation in the Senate seemed almost as promising. FDR had so overwhelming a majority in the upper house that several Democrats were crowded across the aisle into the Republican section. The President figured to lose a few conservative Democrats, but he might make them up with progressive Republicans like Hiram Johnson and Gerald Nye and independents like George Norris.[22] Yet Roosevelt was unlikely to need these, for there were enough Democratic senators who owed their election to him to provide a comfortable margin. If every one of the sixteen Republicans rejected the measure, the opponents would still need more than twice that many Democrats to defeat it.

In the first week, numbers of Democratic senators announced

[20] Stephen Early to FDR, Feb. 8, 1937, FDRL, PSF Supreme Court; Memorandum of Conference with Speaker W. B. Bankhead, Feb. 7, 1937, Lindsay Warren MSS, Southern Historical Collection, University of North Carolina, Box 17; Lawrence Lewis MS Diary, The State Historical Society of Colorado, Denver, Colo., Feb. 12, 1937; New York *American*, Feb. 19, 1937, clipping, Royal Copeland Scrapbooks.

[21] Joe Hendricks to Wellborn Phillips, Jr., Feb. 25, 1937, Hendricks MSS, P. K. Yonge Library of Florida History, Box 2; Bert Lord to B. H. Chernin, Feb. 16, 1937, Lord MSS, Cornell University Collection of Regional History.

[22] J. F. T. O'Connor MS Diary, Feb. 15, 1937, Bancroft Library, University of California.

themselves for the bill, including a phalanx of influential leaders like Majority Leader Joseph T. Robinson of Arkansas, the chairman of the Judiciary Committee, Henry Fountain Ashurst of Arizona, and such potent allies at Pat Harrison of Mississippi, James F. Byrnes, Jr., of South Carolina, and Key Pittman of Nevada. Men of rather conservative disposition, they received the plan with varying degrees of unenthusiasm but supported it out of loyalty to the President and the Democratic Party. More ardent backing came from such New Deal liberals as Hugo Black of Alabama and Sherman Minton of Indiana, both future Supreme Court justices. After assessing the situation, the White House concluded that no more than fifteen Democrats would oppose the bill in the Senate.[23] *Time* reported: "Newshawks who immediately made surveys of Congressional sentiment agreed that the bill would be passed without serious difficulty."[24]

Greeted in the press with anguished cries of outrage, the plan also elicited no little enthusiasm, especially from Roosevelt's admirers. They argued that the proposal was designed not to pack the Court but to "unpack" it, since the Court had been "stuffed" with corporation lawyers in previous Republican regimes.[25] The whole machinery of American government, they asserted, lay at the will of a single justice, Owen Roberts, who, by combining with the Four Horsemen, could nullify the wishes of the people.[26] A number of the bill's proponents charged that the Court

[23] Raymond Clapper MS Diary, LC, Feb. 8, 1937.

[24] *Time,* XXIX (Feb. 15, 1937), 18–19.

[25] William M. Fitch to Stanley Reed, Feb. 16, 1937, National Archives, Dept. of Justice 235868; Vyvian Faye Coxon to Joe Hendricks, Mar. 3, 1937, Hendricks MSS, Box 2.

[26] A Wisconsin man wrote: "It is now possible, under a five to four decision, for one old man (whose mental and physical powers, as any

had usurped its powers; some even denied that there was any constitutional sanction for judicial review.[27] Moreover, they claimed that there was ample historical precedent for altering the size of the Court.[28] Nor would they concede that Roosevelt was plunging the Court into politics; Rep. Thomas R. Amlie, a Wisconsin Progressive, contended: "The fact is that the Supreme Court has always been in politics up to its ears."[29]

Many shared Roosevelt's concern about the age of the justices, a feeling that had been intensified by the best-seller, Robert S. Allen's and Drew Pearson's *The Nine Old Men.*[30] One man wrote Chief Justice Hughes: "Seems to me if I were 75 I would be glad to enjoy life instead of working and taking a job away from some young family man."[31] Some Tennessee lawyers point-

---

honest authority will admit, are more than likely to be in process of deterioration) to nullify the acts of 435 congressmen, 96 senators and the President—all duly elected as the government of the people." C. W. Langlotz to Thomas Amlie, Feb. 12, 1937, Amlie MSS, State Historical Society of Wisconsin, Box 35. See also Henry Ware Allen to the editor, Washington *Post,* May 4, 1937; George Fort Milton to Homer Cummings, Mar. 17, 1937, Milton MSS, LC, Box 20.

[27] Josephus Daniels to Frank Gannett, May 11, 1937, Gannett MSS, Box 16; *Congressional Record,* 75th Cong., 1st Sess., p. 307A.

[28] Lex Green to C. E. Coomes, Feb. 15, 1937, Green MSS, P. K. Yonge Library of Florida History, Box 27.

[29] Thomas R. Amlie to S. A. Jedele, Feb. 12, 1937, Amlie MSS, Box 35.

[30] Thomas Reed Powell to William O. Douglas, n.d., Douglas MSS, LC, Box 20; Herbert Hoover to Charles Evans Hughes, Feb. 19, 1937, Hughes MSS, LC, Box 6; James A. Stone to William T. Evjue, Mar. 17, 1937, Stone MSS, State Historical Society of Wisconsin, Box 28; Thomas R. Amlie to Donald A. Butchart, Mar. 6, 1937, Amlie MSS, Box 36; *The New York Times,* Jan. 27, 1937.

[31] M. A. Hudak to Hughes, Apr. 13, 1937, Hughes MSS, LC, Box 164, For hostility to Hughes, see Chase Osborn to Daniel Willard, Dec. 22, 1937, Osborn MSS, Michigan Historical Collections; Mark Squires to

ed out that a justice of 70 was an adult "before the telephone was invented, he was 35 before the automobile became of importance, and was over 40 before the airplane became a factor in national life. The golden age of gasoline, electricity, chemistry, mass production, radio and education had not in the main begun when the man of 70 had reached the age of 45."[32] A Wisconsin man wrote: "Take it in my own case. I am assured by my acquaintances that I do not look any older than I did fifteen or twenty years ago. That may be true as to looks and mentality, but at my age (seventy seven), any sane man must know that physically I can not measure up to fifteen or twenty years ago. I could not possibly put in working hours that I did when serving in the State Senate eighteen years ago."[33]

Supporters of the plan scoffed at the worshipful attitude opponents took toward the Constitution and the Court. "A constitution is not an idol to be worshipped; it is an instrument of government to be worked," observed Senator Robert J. Bulkley of Ohio.[34] Many doubted the sincerity of the Constitution-worshippers. A South Carolinian noted: "If I got up tomorrow and advocated rigid adherence to the 14th and 15th [Amendments] of the Constitution, the same folks who are yelling 'Constitution' loudly now would fight among themselves for priority in applying the tar and feathers."[35] Henry M. Hart of the Harvard Law

---

R. L. Doughton, Feb. 10, 1937, Doughton MSS, Southern Historical Collection, University of North Carolina.

[32] Nashville *Tennessean,* n.d., clipping in M. H. Berry to Kenneth McKellar, Feb. 10, 1937, McKellar MSS, Memphis Public Library, Memphis, Tenn., Box 202.

[33] Al C. Anderson to Merlin Hull, Feb. 12, 1937, Hull MSS, Box 88.

[34] *Congressional Record,* 75th Cong., 1st Sess., p. 405A.

[35] Edmund P. Grice, Jr. to James F. Byrnes, Feb. 23, 1937, Byrnes

School contested the notion that Supreme Court opinions were like the pronouncements of a Delphic oracle, and Donald Richberg, former chairman of the National Industrial Recovery Board, asserted: "We need to be disillusioned of the idea that putting a black robe upon a man makes him a superior variety of human being."[36] Harold Ickes protested:

> To listen to the clamor, one would think that Moses from Mount Sinai had declared that God Himself had decreed that if and when there should be a Supreme Court of the United States, the number Nine was to be sacred. All that is left to do now is to declare that the Supreme Court was immaculately conceived; that it is infallible; that it is the spiritual descendant of Moses and that the number Nine is three times three, and three stands for the Trinity.[37]

Although such sentiments strengthened the hand of the Administration Democrats in the Senate, the bill encountered even more vigorous opposition, far more than had been anticipated.

MSS, Clemson University, Clemson, S.C. Another Charleston man wrote. "I get a kick out of the hypocritical reverence for the constitution on the part of some of my friends. They often prayed for deliverance from the eighteenth amendment tanked up on a jar of moonshine." Archie P. Owens to the editor, Charleston *News and Courier,* n.d., clipping in Owens to Byrnes, Feb. 21, 1937, *idem.*

[36] Washington *Post,* May 5, 1937; Donald Richberg to Ray Clapper, Feb. 26, 1937, Richberg MSS, LC, Box 2.

[37] Harold Ickes to William Allen White, Feb. 25, 1937, White MSS, LC, Box 186. Ickes was not wide of the mark. A Kansas City attorney who opposed the plan wrote: "The Constitution, by its separation of the trinity of governmental functions, Executive, Legislative and Judicial, vitalized the God concept." W. H. H. Piatt to Robert La Follette, Jr., William Allen White MSS, March 17, 1937, Box 187.

Roosevelt must have expected the defection of Democrats like Carter Glass of Virginia and Josiah Bailey of North Carolina. Much more serious was the rebellion of party regulars like Tom Connally of Texas and of liberal Democrats like Burton K. Wheeler of Montana. The loss of Wheeler was a real stunner. After all, Wheeler had campaigned with Robert M. La Follette in 1924 on the Court reform issue. Since no one could dispute his credentials as a liberal, Wheeler, by denouncing the plan, made it difficult for the President to claim that his adversaries were the same bunch of economic royalists who had fought him in 1936.[38]

In fact, it quickly became apparent that opponents of the plan enjoyed widespread support. Marshaled by the publisher Frank E. Gannett's National Committee to Uphold Constitutional Government, they bombarded congressmen and newspaper editors with remonstrances comparing the President to Stuart tyrants and to European dictators. "Our President evidently has noted the apparent success of Hitler and is aiming at the same dominance," wrote a Saginaw businessman.[39] Opponents pointed out that Roosevelt had failed to suggest in his 1936 campaign either that the country faced a crisis or that he planned to remold the Su-

[38] "The New Deal versus the Old Courts," *Literary Digest*, CXXIII (Feb. 13, 1937), 5–8; Henry Morgenthau Jr. MS Diaries, FDRL, Feb. 15, 1937; Breckinridge Long MS Diary, LC, Feb. 15, 1937.

[39] William B. Mershon to Arthur Vandenberg, Feb. 15, 1937, Mershon MSS, Michigan Historical Collections. See also Merton S. Horrell to Joe Hendricks, Feb. 12, 1937, Hendricks MSS, Box 2; Amy Armour Smith to Rush Holt, Mar. 18, 1937, Holt MSS, University of West Virginia Library, Morgantown, W. Va.; *Constitutional Democracy*, Apr. 5, 1937, copy in Hugh Ike Shott MSS, University of West Virginia Library, Box 38.

preme Court.[40] They argued that the President should seek to
amend the Constitution, and emphasized that it had taken only
ten months to ratify the 21st Amendment.[41] Above all, they protested that Roosevelt was not showing proper regard for the Judiciary. "As a boy I was taught to honor and revere the Supreme
Court of the United States above all things," wrote a New Orleans insurance man.[42] "It seems strange to hear the Supreme
Court discussed like a business, a going concern needing new
capital to expand," commented a Charleston publisher. "We always were taught to think of it, with reverence be it said, as like
the Church, where men selected for their exceptional qualifica-
tions presided as Bishops should."[43] A prominent Catholic lay-

[40] St. Louis *Post-Dispatch,* Apr. 11, 1937; Frank B. De Vine to Jesse
S. Reeves, Reeves MSS, Michigan Historical Collections, Vol. 40. Administration supporters replied that the Court issue had been raised in the
campaign—by Roosevelt's opponents; hence, the President did have a
mandate. Secretary Harold Ickes wrote a Republican editor: "You raised
these issues and the people brought in the verdict against you—an overwhelming verdict. Aren't you estopped from saying now that the question of judicial reform was not raised?" Harold Ickes to William Allen
White, Feb. 20, 1937, White MSS, Box 186. See also A. F. Whitney to
Frank O. Lowden, Apr. 17, 1937, Lowden MSS, University of Chicago
Library, Chicago, Ill., Series 5, Box 25, Folder 2.

[41] Advocates retorted that the amendment process was too slow; they
pointed, in particular, to the long, tedious odyssey of the Child Labor
Amendment. One labor leader objected: "Amendments are O.K., except
we start to save a kid in a So. Car. cotton mill when she is eight—she
is 26 before we get the amendment." George B. Jackson to Joe Hendricks,
Mar. 14, 1937, Hendricks MSS, Box 2. See also Breckinridge Long MS
Diary, Feb. 15, 1937.

[42] A. M. Savage to John H. Overton, Mar. 16, 1937, Overton MSS,
Box 2.

[43] W. W. Ball to "Lily," n.d., Ball MSS, Duke University Library,
Durham, N. Car., July, 1936–Feb., 1937 folder.

man compared the Court's authority to that of the Pope and added: "To all intents and purposes our Supreme Court is infallible. It can not err."[44]

Even friends of the proposal fretted about the deviousness of the President's argument that he was putting it forward because the age of the justices had resulted in crowded dockets, for it seemed obvious that FDR wished to pack the Court with justices of a liberal persuasion. Many took exception to Roosevelt's stress on the age of the justices. Congressmen over seventy were not entranced by the argument that men's faculties are impaired when they reach seventy. Other older people objected that the plan was an assault on the aged, who deserved respect, not opprobrium. One man counseled a Florida congressman: "If you think youth is more competent and reliable than the aged, remember Clemenceau who led France to victory, Chauncey Depew who died at 94 active to the last; Justice Holmes who at 90 gave a Supreme Court decision.

"Reflect how at 84 Hindenburg headed Germany; at 83 Edison was active, and at 86 Elihu Root was doing good work at his office."[45]

Another opponent of the proposal wrote the Washington *Post*: "Between the ages of 70 and 83, Commodore Vanderbilt added one hundred million dollars to his fortune. . . . At 74 Immanuel

[44] Typescript of address by Joseph E. Ransdell, n.d. [July, 1937], Ransdell MSS, Dept. of Archives and Manuscripts, Louisiana State University, Folder 21, Box 3. Almost every Catholic Senator was arrayed against the plan; of all the elements, save for party, that might be associated with a Senator's position on the plan—class, ethnic group, etc.—the most telling was whether or not he was a Catholic.

[45] Vincent P. Smith to Joe Hendricks, Mar. 2, 1937, Hendricks MSS, Box 2.

Kant wrote his 'Anthropology,' the 'Metaphysics of Ethics,' and 'Strife of the Faculties.' . . . Marcus Portius Cato began the study of Greek when a youthful Roman of 80! Goethe at 80, completed 'Faust.' . . . Tennyson wrote his divinely impressive farewell, 'Crossing the Bar' at 83. . . . At 98 Titian painted his historic picture of the 'Battle of Lepanto.' . . . Can you calculate the loss to the world if such as these had been compelled to retire at 70?"[46]

The strategy of the crowded dockets–old age rationale turned out to be a blunder. Before long, the President virtually abandoned this line of argument and came out with his main reason: that the Court was dominated by a set of conservative justices who were making it impossible for liberal government to function.

This emphasis appealed to many of Roosevelt's New Deal followers, but others bristled at any attempt to alter the Court. They charged the President with tampering with the institutions established by the Founding Fathers. Although the number of justices had been changed several times before, many believed that the Constitution specified nine members. One writer encountered an elderly lady who protested. "If nine judges were enough for

[46] The Vicar to the editor, Mar. 10, 1937, Washington *Post,* Mar. 12, 1937. A Missouri country editor urged: "Let these men serve until they are taken by their maker or resign. . . . They have lived the span of life allotted them by Him, if they live longer it is because He has work for them to do." Raymond Lloyd to James F. Byrnes, Feb. 17, 1937, Byrnes MSS. A North Carolinian assured his elderly Congressman: "I am glad to say that your own constituents do not feel that a man is mentally decrepit at the age of seventy." Waller D. Brown to R. L. Doughton, Feb. 10, 1937, Doughton MSS. Admirers of Justice Brandeis resented the plan as an implied slur at the octogenarian justice.

George Washington, they should be enough for President Roosevelt. I don't see why he needs fifteen."[47] In vain, supporters of the bill retorted that the Founding Fathers had been revolutionaries and that the opponents were attempting to escape modern problems by evoking nostalgia for a mythical past.

Still other critics like the historian James Truslow Adams valued the Judiciary as "the sole bulwark of our personal liberties." "If a President tries to take away our freedom of speech, if a Congress takes away our property unlawfully, if a State legislature, as in the recent case of Louisiana under the dictatorship of Huey Long, takes away the freedom of the press, who is to save us except the Courts?" he asked.[48] "If I were a Hebrew I would be scared green," asserted a Detroit businessman. "If I were a Negro I'd hate to have my precious amendment taken away from me—the one that put me on an equal footing with whites, thanks to Mr. Lincoln."[49] On the other hand, Southerners frequently

[47] Richard L. Neuberger, "America Talks Court," *Current History,* XLVI (June, 1937), 35.

[48] Address, Mar. 8, 1937, Station WOR, J. T. Adams MSS, Columbia University Library, New York, N.Y.

[49] Harvey Campbell to Arthur Vandenberg, Mar. 11, 1937, Vandenberg MSS, Clements Library, University of Michigan. See also Hugh L. Elsbree to Daniel Reed, Oct. 3, 1958, Reed MSS, Cornell University Collection of Regional History, Box 14; William F. Riley to his father, Mar. 3, 1937, in Riley to Clyde Herring, July 7, 1937, Riley MSS, University of Iowa Library, Iowa City, Iowa, Box 1; Oswald Garrison Villard to Maury Maverick, May 7, 1937, Villard MSS, Houghton Library, Harvard University, Cambridge, Mass. Advocates denied that the Court, and especially the Four Horsemen, had safeguarded civil liberties. Maury Maverick wrote: "If you look at the cases on sedition, espionage and the rest, . . . the courts declared pretty nearly every silly law constitutional during and following the World War. There was not much protection

warned that the Court was a bastion of white supremacy. "Our
very social and racial integrity rest behind these 'checks and bal-
ances,' " a constituent wrote the Louisiana senators.[50] "Voices cry
from every Confederate grave," declared another.[51]

So intensely did opponents object to the plan that a number of
Democratic senators searched desperately for some device that
would free them of the need to commit themselves. In particular,
the freshman Democrats who had been swept into office in the
Roosevelt tidal wave in 1936 looked for a way that would save
them from voting for a scheme which many found repugnant
and which they knew outraged many of their constituents, if they
could do so without breaking openly with the President. Typical
of these freshman Democrats were Prentiss Brown of Michigan,
who took a resolutely noncommittal stance; Senator Andrews of
Florida, who told his son: "It will be my policy, right on, not to
commit myself to any particular course with regard to the
Courts"; and John H. Overton of Louisiana, who raised straddling to an art.[52] Overton's standard release stated: "The impor-

---

of civil liberties in this country." Maverick to John I. Palmer, Jan. 18,
1937, Maury Maverick MSS, Archives, University of Texas Library,
Austin, Tex., Box 5.

[50] Virgil Murdoch Rich to Senators Overton and Ellender, Feb. 10,
1937, Overton MSS, Box 2.

[51] Edith Dickeymann to James F. Byrnes, n.d., Byrnes MSS.

[52] Andrews to Charles Andrews, Jr., Feb. 26, 1937, Andrews MSS,
Box 51; Charles O. Andrews to Hamilton Holt, Mar. 10, 1937, Holt
MSS, Mills Memorial Library, Rollins College, Winter Park, Fla.; Detroit *News*, Feb. 6, 28, 1937. For other indications of straddling, or concern for public opinion, see F. Ryan Duffy to William B. Rubin, Feb. 11,
1937, Rubin MSS, State Historical Society of Wisconsin, Box 11; J. F. T.
O'Connor MS Diary, Feb. 18, 1937; Portland *Press-Herald,* Feb. 6, 1937,

tance of the subject, its many aspects, the high source of the recommendation and the contrariety of opinion throughout the United States suggest to me that the proper course is to with-hold any definite conclusion until the matter has been more thoroughly investigated, discussed and considered."[53] To one constituent, Senator Overton explained: "You state that you note that I am following Polonius' advice to 'reserve thy judgment.' I am going farther than this and, to paraphrase another precept of his, I am with respect to this matter, giving every man my ear and none, as yet, my voice."[54]

With the Democrats divided, the Republicans, at the urging of the canny Minority Leader, Charles McNary of Oregon, re-solved to keep quiet and thus avoid offering an occasion that might re-unite the Democrats.[55] On the day after the President sent his message, Republican Senator Arthur Vandenberg of Michigan recorded in his diary: "This morning ex-President Hoover phoned me from the Waldorf-Astoria in New York, eager to jump into the fray. . . . Now here is one of the tragedies of life. Hoover is still 'poison'—(the right or the wrong of it does not matter). [William]Borah, McNary and I had a con-ference at 11 o'clock. Borah is prepared to lead this fight; but he insisted that there is no hope if it is trade-marked in advance as a

clipping, Wallace White MSS, LC, Box 81; Fred Crawford to H. A. Douglas, Mar. 17, 1937, Crawford MSS, Michigan Historical Collections.

[53] Mimeographed copy, John H. Overton MSS, Box 2.

[54] Overton to Fayette C. Ewing, Feb. 20, 1937, *idem.*

[55] Karl A. Lamb, "The Opposition Party as Secret Agent: Republicans and the Court Fight, 1937," *Papers of the Michigan Academy of Science, Arts, and Letters*, Vol. XLVI (1961).

'Hoover fight' or a 'Republican fight.' McNary emphatically agreed. As a matter of fact, this already was my own attitude."[56] Men like Vandenberg, McNary, and Borah, senator from Idaho, managed to get most national GOP leaders to abide by the strategy of silence, although Hoover would not go along.[57] While the Republicans, by their restraint, were encouraging Democratic dissension, they held their own lines. Although the Administration had expected the support of some progressive Republicans, in the end every one of the sixteen Republican senators, including Johnson and Nye, rejected the bill.

The opponents made the most of the opportunity offered by the public hearings before the Senate Judiciary Committee. They led off with their most important witness, Senator Wheeler, who began with a discursive, disarming statement that gradually worked around toward the Administration's contention that aged justices were unable to keep abreast of their work. With a dramatic flourish, Wheeler then unfolded a letter from Chief Justice Charles Evans Hughes. The Chief Justice denied that the Court was behind in its business or that more justices would increase efficiency. Instead, he asserted, "there would be more judges to hear, more judges to confer, more judges to discuss, more judges to be convinced and to decide."[58] Hughes's unanticipated contri-

[56] Arthur Vandenberg MS Diary, Clements Library, University of Michigan, Feb. 6, 1937.

[57] Herbert Hoover to Frank O. Lowden, Feb. 6, 1937, Lowden MSS, Series I, Box 58, Folder 5; Arthur M. Hyde to Paul Shoup, May 12, 1937, Shoup MSS, Stanford University Library, Stanford, Calif., Box 1. Too much has often been made of the Republican strategy of silence; men like Vandenberg spoke out after only a brief period of reticence.

[58] U.S. Senate Committee on the Judiciary, 75th Cong., 1st Sess., *Reorganization of the Federal Judiciary*, Hearings on S. 1392 (Washington:

bution not only effectively rebutted the President's crowded dockets argument, but suggested that henceforth Roosevelt, in pushing his proposal, would encounter not only the wily Wheeler but the formidable figure of the Chief Justice.

The Administration made the mistake of presenting its case briefly, and most of the hearings served to publicize the views of the opposition. The President's former aide, Raymond Moley, clergymen, law school deans, and spokesmen for farm organizations all testified against the measure. Professor Erwin Griswold of Harvard Law School protested that "this bill obviously is not playing the game. There are at least two ways of getting rid of judges," he observed. "One is to take them out and shoot them, as they are reported to do in at least one other country. The other way is more genteel, but no less effective. They are kept on the public payroll but their votes are canceled."[59]

Despite all the antagonism, it still seemed highly likely in the last week of March that the President's proposal would be adopted. Many of those who were skeptical of the scheme nonetheless did not want the Court to continue to invalidate New Deal laws,

---

Government Printing Office, 1937), Part 3, p. 491. Supporters of the plan retorted that if the Court was up to date on its calendar it was only because, ever since the enactment of a 1925 statute, the Court had been refusing to hear cases it should have heard. A federal district court judge from Los Angeles wrote: "I have never seen any logic in catching up with court calendars by shutting off the right to ask for justice, and that, in plain truth, is just what has been done. It is child's talk to say that the business of the court cannot be apportioned among fifteen so that more and better work can be turned out than through a court of nine." Albert Lee Stephens to William McAdoo, May 21, 1937, McAdoo MSS, LC, Box 435. But see Stanley Reed to FDR, Feb. 26, 1937, FDRL OF 10–F.

[59] U.S. Senate, Committee on the Judiciary, *Hearings on S. 1392*, Pt. 4, p. 767.

and if faced with a choice between Roosevelt's plan and the
strangling of the New Deal, they would be likely to go along
with the President. Roosevelt was certain to win unless Democratic senators, especially the freshmen, deserted him in droves,
and it did not seem well-advised to break with a man who had
been given so emphatic an endorsement just a few months before.
Senator Andrews' son scolded his father: "I have noticed a decided dissatisfaction among the laymen for your straddling attitude regarding the Supreme Court. . . . I do not see how you can
stand to go against the President and his Supreme Court proposal. Your being in Washington you cannot realize the absolute
necessity of patronage and you have not gotten one little bit and
you have got to have it. This Supreme Court proposal is the first
test that will be placed upon your loyalty to the Democratic
party. A year from now you might afford to 'bolt,' but right now
I do not see how you can afford to have them place you on the
first go-round as a 'bolter.' "[60]

A Michigan voter stated even more bluntly:

> I had never heard of Prentiss M. Brown until the last election,
> when I learned that a man by that name had been nominated for
> the United States Senate on the Democratic ticket.
>
> So I voted for Brown, not because he was Brown, but because
> he merely happened to be the candidate on the Roosevelt ballot,
> and I wanted to send to Washington every man possible to aid
> our President. . . .
>
> Now I read with amazement . . . this Senator Brown as saying
> that he has not made up his mind regarding just how he'll vote
> on the proposal to change the Supreme Court.

[60] Charles Andrews, Jr., to Charles O. Andrews, Mar. 11, 1937, Andrews MSS, Box 51.

Why does Senator Brown think we made him Senator Brown and sent him to Washington? We sent him there to support Roosevelt. Brown as Brown doesn't have to do any thinking or make any decisions. If he merely follows the policies outlined by our President he will be doing all the voters who voted for him will require.[61]

Men like Brown and Andrews continued to probe for a satisfactory compromise, but when it came to the showdown they figured to be on Roosevelt's side. At the end of March, *Time* wrote: "Last week the stanchest foes of the President's Plan were privately conceding that, if he chose to whip it through, the necessary votes were already in his pockets."[62] The undecided senators might not like the plan, but they could not justify frustrating the President while the Court persisted in mowing down New Deal legislation.

But the Court itself had some big surprises in store. On March 29, in a 5–4 decision in which Justice Roberts joined the majority, the Court upheld a minimum wage statute from the state of Washington which to most people seemed identical to the New York law it had wiped out in the *Tipaldo* case less than a year before.[63] Two weeks later, Roberts joined in a series of 5–4 decisions which found the National Labor Relations Act constitutional.[64] On May 24, the Court validated the Social Security law.[65] These decisions marked an historic change in constitutional

[61] F.R.L. to the editor, Mar. 2, 1937, Detroit *News.*

[62] *Time,* XXIX (Apr. 5, 1937), 13.

[63] West Coast Hotel Company *v.* Parrish, 300 U.S. 379 (1937).

[64] The most important case was National Labor Relations Board *v.* Jones & Laughlin Steel Corporation, 301 U.S. 1 (1937).

[65] Steward Machine Company *v.* Davis, 301 U.S. 548 (1937); Helvering *v.* Davis, 301 U.S. 619 (1937).

doctrine. The Court was now stating that the state and federal governments had a whole range of powers which this same tribunal had been saying for the past two years these governments did not have.

The crucial development was the switch of Justice Roberts, which altered a 5–4 margin against New Deal legislation to a 5–4 edge in favor. Some analysts have argued that Roberts did not change at all. They explain that his response in earlier cases resulted from his unwillingness to rule on questions not properly brought before the Court.[66] This contention is not altogether unreasonable with respect to the relation of the *Tipaldo* to the *Parrish* decision, but if the Social Security opinions are compared to the rail pension ruling, or the Wagner Act opinions with the *Carter* decision, it seems unmistakable that the Court, and specifically Mr. Justice Roberts, had shifted ground.

Commentators differed, too, about why Justice Roberts joined the liberal majority. Some believed that Roberts had been brought in line by Chief Justice Hughes with the deliberate intent of defeating the President's plan by removing its main justification. A columnist asserted: "No insider doubts that the whole change of trend represented in the decisions was solely the work of Mr. Hughes. Everyone gives Mr. Hughes credit for arguing Associate Justice Roberts into position."[67] Others thought that Roberts had merely followed the election returns.[68] Roosevelt's Court

[66] Merlo Pusey, *Charles Evans Hughes* (2 vols., New York, 1951), II, 757, 766–772; Felix Frankfurter, "Mr. Justice Roberts," *University of Pennsylvania Law Reviews,* CIV (Dec., 1955), 313–316. But see Edward F. Prichard, Jr., to the editor, Boston *Herald,* Apr. 2, 1937, copy in Theodore Green MSS, LC, Box 32.

[67] Paul Mallon, "Purely Confidential," Detroit *News,* Apr. 13, 1937.

[68] At least one justice did not anticipate that Roosevelt would win so

proposal could not have been alone responsible, for the *Parrish* decision was reached before the President sent his message to Congress, although it was not handed down until afterwards.

Many observers, especially supporters of the plan, had no doubt that the Court had altered its views, and that it had done so because it had been baptized "in the waters of public opinion."[69] After the *Parrish* decision, one correspondent asked William Allen White: "Didn't the Welshman on the Supreme Court do a pretty job of amending the Constitution yesterday?[70] George Fort Milton, the Tennessee editor and historian, observed: "The Supreme Court thing is quite amazing. Mr. Roberts changed his mind and so a law unconstitutional for New York is constitutional for the State of Washington."[71] Justice Roberts, said a national Democratic leader, "performed that marvelous somersault in mid-air. One day Mr. Roberts is at one side of the tent—the next day he grasps the trapeze, makes a far swing, turns a double somersault and lands on the other side of the tent. But there [is] no telling when he will swing back again."[72]

The switch by Roberts had ironic consequences. In one sense,

------

handsomely; a number of judges might well have believed until that point that they were defending the people against an overbearing tyrant. The election results must have been a jolt. See Willis Van Devanter to Dennis Flynn, Oct. 19, 1936; Van Devanter to Mrs. John W. Lacey, Nov. 2, 1936, Van Devanter MSS, LC, Vol. 52.

[69] Detroit *News,* Apr. 13, 1937; Thomas Amlie to Mr. and Mrs. E. J. Klema, July 6, 1937, Amlie MSS, Box 39; J. F. T. O'Connor MS Diary, Apr. 12, 1937.

[70] Tom Lewis to William Allen White, Mar. 30, 1937, White MSS, Box 187.

[71] Milton to Joseph Greenbaum, Apr. 1, 1937, Milton MSS, Box 20.

[72] Emma Guffey Miller, "Speech—Louisville [1937]," Miller MSS, Folder 36, Schlesinger Library, Radcliffe College.

it gave Roosevelt the victory he wanted, for the Court was now approving New Deal legislation.[73] But in another way, Roberts' "somersault" gravely damaged the chances of the Court plan. By eliminating the critical need for changing the membership of the bench, it erased the most important justification for the President's bill. Why change the Court now that you had the kind of decisions that you wanted? As someone said, "A switch in time saved nine."[74]

This argument became even more compelling when on the morning of May 18, while the President was breakfasting in bed, a messenger arrived at the White House with a letter from Justice Van Devanter announcing his resignation from the bench. Van Devanter's action was widely believed to have been the result of counsel from Senators Borah and Wheeler. Borah lived in the same apartment house on Connecticut Avenue; the two were on "Hello, Bill" and "Hello, Willis" terms.[75] The "conversion"

[73] Some conservatives believed that the Court's reversal had defeated the bill, but that too great a price had been paid. Newton Baker wrote: "The change of position by Mr. Justice Roberts is profoundly disturbing and distressing. I think the Court is already saved from the President's proposal, but how much of the old dignity and disinterestedness of the Court will remain as a tradition is a very serious question." Baker to John H. Clarke, June 9, 1937, Baker MSS, LC, Box 60.

[74] Edward Corwin to Homer Cummings, May 19, 1937, Corwin MSS, Princeton University Library, Princeton, N.J.; Raymond Clapper MS Diary, June 10, 1937.

[75] Willis Van Devanter to FDR, May 18, 1937, Van Devanter MSS, Vol. 54; *Time*, XXIX (May 31, 1937), 17; Stephen Tyree Early, Jr., "James Clark McReynolds and the Judicial Process," unpublished Ph.D. dissertation, University of Virginia, 1954, p. 102. Three months later, Borah wrote: "I made no effort to persuade anyone to get off the Supreme bench. I think I have a fair amount of nerve, but I would not

of Roberts had given Roosevelt a 5–4 majority; soon he would be able to name someone to take Van Devanter's place and have the opportunity for a 6–3 margin.

Since it appeared that Roosevelt had won substantially what he wanted, he was now urged to call off the fight. "Why," it was asked, "shoot the bridegroom after a shotgun wedding?"[76] The *Parrish* and Wagner decisions turned some Senators against the plan, and encouraged others to press for compromise. Prentiss Brown stated that the switch of the Court took "a good deal of the ground work from under the arguments for the court bill and I believe it will open the way for friends and opponents to re-approach the issue."[77] By the end of April, the two sides were roughly even. One poll showed forty-four senators in favor, forty-seven opposed, four doubtful, with one seat vacant. The Social Security opinions and Van Devanter's resignation tipped the balance against the six-judge bill; thereafter, opponents held a narrow edge.[78]

---

undertake such a job as that." Borah to A. A. Lewis, Aug. 11, 1937, Borah MSS, LC, Box 414. The editor of the Boston *Herald* offered a different explanation: "That is a beautiful little controversy between the President and the C. J. Don't you suppose that Charles the Baptist persuaded Van Devanter to withdraw? Aren't the honors with the Chief Justice to date, rather than with the President?" Frank Buxton to William Allen White, June 8, 1937, White MSS, Box 189.

[76] *Time,* XXIX (June 7, 1937), 13.

[77] Saginaw *Daily News,* Apr. 13, 1937, clipping, Prentiss Brown Scrapbooks, St. Ignace, Mich. (privately held).

[78] Detroit *News,* May 19, 1937; Frank V. Cantwell, "Public Opinion and the Legislative Process," *American Political Science Review,* LV (1946), 933–935. An advocate of the bill wrote: "The resignation of Justice Van Devanter has somewhat altered the situation and it is doubtful if the plan will pass the Senate with[out] some modification." Henry

Many of the Roosevelt leaders in Congress wanted to drop the whole project, but others argued that justices who could switch so easily in his favor could just as easily jump back once the pressure was off. One of the President's aides said: "No man's land now is Roberts land."[79] The Scripps Howard columnist Raymond Clapper noted in his diary that Roosevelt's press secretary had told him "that president is going ahead with fight—that don't know how long Hughes can keep Roberts liberal or how long Hughes will stay so."[80] Others reasoned that the switch of the Court had proven what FDR had been saying all along: there was nothing wrong with the Constitution, only with the Court. And if enlightenment was such a good thing, why not have more of it?[81] Senator Theodore Green of Rhode Island de-

---

G. Teigan to Ross Blythe, May 20, 1937, Teigan MSS, Minnesota Historical Society, St. Paul, Minn., Box 16. On the same morning that Van Devanter resigned, the Senate Judiciary Committee voted, 10–8, to reject the plan.

[79] Raymond Clapper MS Diary, Apr. 20, 1937.

[80] *Ibid.*, May 24, 1937. One White House memorandum concluded: "The President has attained the most difficult of his *objectives,* i.e., the liberalization of the interpretation of the Constitution. He has yet to obtain these two objectives: (a) insurance of the continuity of that liberalism and (b) a more perfect judicial mechanism for giving a maximum of justice in a minimum of time." FDRL, PSF Supreme Court.

[81] Address by Lewis Schwellenbach to Labor's Non-Partisan League, Minneapolis, Minn., Apr. 19, 1937, Schwellenbach MSS, LC, Box 1; Augustus L. and Alice B. Richards to Augustine Lonergan, Apr. 13, 1937, Richards MSS, Cornell University Collection of Regional History; Josephus Daniels to Joseph O'Mahoney, Apr. 7, 1937, O'Mahoney MSS, University of Wyoming Library, Laramie, Wyo.; William McAdoo to Walter Jones, Apr. 1, 1937; McAdoo MSS, Box 433; William Chilton to Roscoe Briggs, Apr. 1, 1937, Chilton MSS, University of West Virginia Library, Box 12; Philadephia *Record,* Apr. 20, 1937, clipping, Frank Murphy Collection, University of Michigan Law School.

clared: "Again we learn that the Constitution is what Mr. Justice Roberts says it is. So what we need is not amendments to the Constitution, but a sufficient number of judges to construe it broadly, lest one man's mistaken opinion may decide the fate of a nation."[82]

Furthermore, Roosevelt believed the country was with him. After all, he had won a decisive victory only a half year before. "Why compromise?" Jim Farley asked. "The Democratic senators were elected on the basis of supporting the President's program. It is up to them to back it now."[83] To be sure, mail ran heavily against the bill, but since attitudes toward the plan divided sharply on class lines, and upper income groups were more articulate, this was not surprising. Members of Congress noted that opponents of the proposal often wrote on lithographed and embossed stationery, and when they analyzed their mail, they frequently found, too, that adverse letters came overwhelmingly from Republicans who in the recent campaign had been noisy but outnumbered.[84] If the press denounced the plan, 80 per cent of

[82] Statement of Theodore Francis Green, Green MSS, Box 32. George Fort Milton commented on the Wagner decisions: "It would be quite an unsafe thing to depend on the continuance of the present Robertian attachment as an anchor for a new constitutional attitude of the Government. Logically, Roberts' shift demonstrates so clearly the correctness of the Administration's position that the Constitution is all right; all that was wrong was an uncontemporarily-minded majority of the Court." George Fort Milton to Homer Cummings, Apr. 14, 1937, Milton MSS, Box 20.

[83] *Time,* XXIX (May 24, 1937), 9.

[84] Holland (Mich.) *Sentinel,* Feb. 16, 1937, clipping, Arthur Vandenberg Scrapbooks; Harold Ball to Joe Hendricks, Mar. 8, 1937, Hendricks MSS, Box 2; George Baldwin to Pat McCarran, June 2, 1937, McCarran MSS, Nevada State Museum, Carson City, Nev., File 672; B. H. Chernin

editorial writers had been against FDR in 1936, and look what
had happened on Election Day. True, the polls also showed a
small margin unfavorable to the bill, but remember how wrong
the *Literary Digest* canvass had been a few months before. Only
one significant election had been held since the President sent his
message, and in that race a congressional seat in Texas had been
won by a candidate committed to the plan, a newcomer named
Lyndon B. Johnson.

Yet another reason compelled Roosevelt to push ahead. Although he could name a new judge to the Van Devanter vacancy,
it was understood that he had promised the next opening on the
bench to Senator Robinson. He could hardly avoid choosing the
Majority Leader without inciting a Senate uprising. Yet Robinson was a 65-year-old conservative. If appointing Robinson was
to be the climax of his campaign to bring young, liberal men
to the Court, the enterprise would turn out to be a fiasco. It
seemed more necessary than ever to balance the expected Robinson appointment by creating vacancies for liberal justices.

Well before the end of May, however, Roosevelt's lieutenants

---

to Bert Lord, Feb. 12, 1937, Lord MSS; M. E. Hennessy, "Round About,"
Boston *Globe,* clipping, n.d., David I. Walsh Scrapbooks, Holy Cross
College Library, Worcester, Mass.; William Gibbs McAdoo to H. Hyer
Whiting, Mar. 15, 1937, McAdoo MSS, Box 432. When Senator Green
received a monster telegram from members of the Rhode Island bar op-
posing the plan, he had the signatures analyzed; of those who could be
identified, 213 were Republicans, seven Democrats. Memorandum, Theodore Green MSS, Box 35. A Baltimore man wrote Senator Byrnes: "On
my bended knees, I beg of you not to place the American people at the
mercy of a man who seems to have only the interests of the lower classes
at heart. . . . Please before it is too late consider the interests of your
own class." Anon. to James F. Byrnes, Feb. 19, 1937, Byrnes MSS.

in Congress had to face up to the fact that they simply did not have the votes. One leader confided that five polls of the Senate had all come out with the same result: defeat.[85] Still Roosevelt temporized. Not until the night of June 3 at a two-hour conference at the White House did the President finally agree to permit Senator Robinson to seek a compromise. Acting as Roosevelt's broker, the Majority Leader worked out a revised bill which authorized the President to appoint an additional justice for each member of the Court who was 75; no more than one could be named in any calendar year. This meant that Roosevelt, besides filling the Van Devanter opening, might add four new judges, and this total could not be reached before 1941. By the time this measure had been pieced together, the President had lost much of the advantage of his willingness to bargain; deals that would have been appealing in April were no longer so by late May or June. "It is impossible today for the President to pass his six Judge Bill, and I seriously doubt whether he can pass a two Judge Bill," Senator Vandenberg claimed.[86]

By June, the fight had become very bitter, and although one opponent conceded that Robinson's compromise would win, the issue was close. The Senate divided so evenly that some predicted that when the roll was finally called, the outcome would be a tie which could be broken only by the vote of Vice-President John Nance Garner. The Vice-President had made no secret of the fact that he disapproved of the plan. When the President's message was being read in February, he had held his nose and pointed

[85] Lindsay Warren to A. D. McLean, May 23, 1937, Warren MSS, Box 17.

[86] Arthur Vandenberg to William E. Evans, May 24, 1937, "Personal and Confidential," Vandenberg MSS.

thumbs down. Now, in mid-June, Garner packed his bags and
left to go fishing in Texas. Never before had he departed from
Washington while Congress was in session.[87]

Two days after Garner decamped, the Senate Judiciary Committee published an adverse report which stunned Washington
by the harshness of its censure of the President's plan. The report, signed by members of the President's own party, stated: "It
is a measure which should be so emphatically rejected that its
parallel will never again be presented to the free representatives
of the free people of America."[88] The columnist Ray Clapper
noted in his diary: "Bitter document, extremely rough. . . . It
reads almost like a bill of impeachment."[89]

Everything now hung on the persuasive powers of Senator

[87] Clippings in Scrapbook 13, John Nance Garner Papers, Archives,
University of Texas Library. It created a deep rift between Garner and
the White House circle. Raymond Clapper noted in his diary that Roosevelt's press secretary, Stephen Early, agreed with him "that Garner is at
bottom of a lot of White House trouble now. Early says must be remem-
bered that he is a millionaire and he has his goats and nut trees—is a
plantation man." Raymond Clapper MS Diary, Aug. 3, 1937. See also,
Joseph Guffey to FDR, July 29, 1939, Guffey MSS, Washington and
Jefferson College Library, Washington, Pa.

[88] U.S. Senate, Committee on the Judiciary, 75th Cong., 1st Sess.,
Report No. 711 (Washington: Government Printing Office, 1937), p. 23.

[89] Raymond Clapper MS Diary, June 14, 1937. Another political column noted: "The fury with which President Roosevelt's fellow Democrats on the Senate Judiciary Committee damned the New Deal's court
plan today amazed this politically sophisticated capital. . . . What was
not expected was the revelation that a group of Democratic Senators
would scourge themselves into an emotional frenzy to denounce a head
of their party who had carried 46 States only last November." John
O'Donnell and Doris Fleeson, "Capitol Stuff," New York *Daily News*,
June 15, 1937, clipping, Royal Copeland Scrapbooks.

Robinson. A leader of his party, Joe Robinson had been chosen Democratic Vice-Presidential nominee in 1928, and in his many years on the Hill, he had put a number of men in obligation to him. A man of overbearing manner, he might intimidate some of the freshmen senators into going along. Besides, as *Time* noted: "Just as an expectant mother commands a certain ethereal prestige above other women, so Joe Robinson, as an expectant Justice of the Supreme Court, has become since Justice Van Devanter's retirement a sort of Super-Senator with a prestige all his own among his colleagues."[90] Through the sheer force of his own personality, the Majority Leader might be able to get Roosevelt those few uncommitted votes that could mean the difference between victory and defeat. Without Robinson, the President would be undone.

In the steaming month of July, the great debate in the Senate opened with no one certain how the final roll call would go. At the start of the debate, Administration leaders claimed a minimum of fifty-four senators, and on July 7, the Washington bureau of the Portland (Maine) *Press Herald* reported: "General opinion is the substitute will pass, and sooner than expected, since votes enough to pass it seem apparent, and the opposition cannot filibuster forever."[91] That same day, Hiram Johnson informed a confidant: "They have the votes at present to put it over."[92] Three days later, Senator Kenneth McKellar of Tennessee wrote: "I am inclined to the belief that the bill substan-

---

[90] *Time,* XXIX (June 14, 1937), 11.

[91] Press Herald Bureau, Washington, Portland *Press Herald,* July 7, 1937, clipping, Wallace White MSS, Box 81.

[92] Hiram Johnson to Garret W. McEnerney, July 7, 1937, Johnson MSS.

tially as advocated by the President's friends in the Senate will be passed."[93] With at least forty senators arrayed against the plan, opponents asserted that a filibuster could forestall a roll call indefinitely. But there were risks in resorting to a filibuster, especially when Roosevelt's foes purported to be embattled democrats. *Business Week* lamented: "Too many of them are not willing to run a real, organized filibuster. Too many of them are uncertain whether they would be justified in the eyes of their constituents."[94] Yet neither could the Administration be sure of its own ranks; many of the freshmen senators seemed shaky. On July 10, the Associated Press found seventeen votes still in doubt. On July 12, Senator Edward Burke of Nebraska circulated privately a tally which showed that a switch of four votes would produce a tie.[95]

To hold the waverers in line, Senator Robinson ran the debate with a whip hand. He invoked seldom-used rules to ward off the possibility of a filibuster, and even threatened continuous sessions, although members protested that such an ordeal would take its toll of the Senate, more than a third of which was over sixty.[96] Tempers grew short in the murderous Washington heat. Senator McNary wrote home: "We are having a hot spell and the weather is just as hot as ———, at least as hot as I think it is."[97]

[93] Kenneth McKellar to Charles T. Pennebaker, July 10, 1937, McKellar MSS, Box 97.

[94] "How to Bust Court Filibuster?" *Business Week* (July 17, 1937), 14–15.

[95] Memorandum, Frank Gannett MSS, Box 16.

[96] Detroit *Free Press,* July 11, 1937.

[97] McNary to Mrs. W. T. Stolz, July 10, 1937, McNary MSS, LC, Box 1.

On the opening day of debate, Robinson left the floor feeling ill. "No more questions today," he said. "Goodby!"[98] Several days later, the Majority Leader, in an angry exchange with an opposition senator, once again felt pain in his chest and had to leave the chamber. He did not appear on the Senate floor the next day. The following morning, his maid knocked on the door of his apartment and got no response. When she entered, she found Senator Robinson sprawled on the floor, dead.

The death of Joe Robinson doomed all hopes for Roosevelt's plan. "The Court issue went with Joe," concluded a Florida congressman.[99] "I think the death of Robinson will have a marked effect upon the Congress," wrote a former governor of North Carolina, "and I do not think that Robert E. Lee sustained a greater loss in the death of Stonewall Jackson than Roosevelt has lost in the death of Robinson."[100] A Minnesota editor reflected: "It is not unlikely that the death of Senator Robinson will be the turning point in the President's career."[101]

To anxious senators, already on edge from the strain of the long session, it seemed that Death had intervened to decide the fate of the Republic.[102] A Washington column reported: "The sudden passing of Robinson has brought the pressure of wives, families and physicians on many senators to hasten their depar-

---

[98] *Time,* XXX (July 26, 1937), 10.

[99] Lex Green to J. H. Scales, July 19, 1937, Green MSS, Box 27.

[100] O. Max Gardner to B. B. Gossett, July 16, 1937, Gardner MSS, Southern Historical Collection, University of North Carolina, Box 15.

[101] Elmer Ellsworth Adams to Theo Christianson, July 16, 1937, Adams MSS, Minnesota Historical Society, Box 42.

[102] Middletown *Times Herald,* July 15, 1937, clipping, Royal Copeland Scrapbooks.

ture from the sweltering capital."[103] Earlier in the session, one senator had died; two others were undergoing treatment at the Naval Hospital. Senator Copeland warned that, as a doctor, he could see on the faces of others in the chamber the same tell-tale signs of imminent death he had discerned in Senator Robinson's countenance in the past week. Senator Wheeler shouted that Robinson's death was a direct result of Roosevelt's Court bill. "I beseech the President to drop the fight lest he appear to fight against God."[104] (One correspondent wrote Wheeler: "Your bad taste is surpassed only by your conceit in assuming the role of God's spokesman.")[105]

On the train returning from Senator Robinson's funeral in Little Rock, every compartment housed a caucus. In one compartment, three of the freshman senators decided that the game was over. When he returned to Washington, Prentiss Brown called together eight freshman Democrats, including Senators Overton and Andrews, who held the balance of power. After a two-hour conference on July 20, they marched across the hall in the Senate Office Building to Vice-President Garner's office to announce that they would vote to recommit the bill.[106] That did it. Hiram Johnson explained: "After the self-delivery of the freshmen Senators, we had fifty or fifty-one votes, but we did not have them until

[103] Doris Fleeson and John O'Donnell, "Capitol Stuff," Buffalo *Courier Press,* July 16, 1937, clipping, Royal Copeland Scrapbooks.

[104] *The New York Times,* July 15, 1937.

[105] *Ibid.,* July 16, 1937.

[106] Detroit *Free Press,* July 21, 1937; Detroit *News,* July 21, 23, 1937, clippings, Prentiss Brown Scrapbooks; interview, Prentiss Brown, St. Ignace, Mich., July 7, 1965; Frank Gannett to J. P. Simmons, July 23, 1937, Gannett MSS, Box 3A; John H. Overton to Richard W. Leche *et al.,* July 22, 1937, Overton MSS.

then."[107] The struggle ended so abruptly that Republicans who had worked for months on speeches they were to give in the Great Debate never had a chance to deliver them.[108]

But for FDR, all was not lost. Not only did he have a Court which was ruling in favor of the constitutionality of New Deal laws, but he still had the right to appoint someone to the vacancy created by Van Devanter's retirement. Once more, he kept the Capitol in suspense. Day after day passed without his making a move. It was even suspected that he would not choose anyone until after the Senate had recessed. Then one day, again taking the country by surprise, he scrawled a name on a Court commission and sent it by messenger up to the Hill. The name was that of Senator Hugo Black of Alabama.

No appointment could have been better calculated to infuriate his opponents. Black had been an enthusiastic supporter of the Court plan, and he was one of the leading liberals in Congress. But senators who wanted to reject him could not bring themselves to turn down one of their own members. Despite rumors, subsequently confirmed, that Black had been a member of the Ku Klux Klan, the nomination went through fairly easily. Just a few weeks after Roosevelt had apparently been beaten, he had scored another victory.[109]

Black was only the first of a series of judges Roosevelt was

---

[107] Johnson to John Francis Neylan, July 24, 1937, Johnson MSS.

[108] Detroit *Free Press,* July 23, 1937.

[109] Raymond Clapper MS Diary, Aug. 4, 1937; Hiram Johnson to Lulu Leppo, Oct. 8, 1937, Johnson MSS; William Borah to Jess Hawley, Aug. 16, 1937, Borah MSS, Box 412; Rev. Edward Lodge Curran to Louis Brandeis, Oct. 6, 1937, Brandeis MSS, University of Louisville Law School Library, Louisville, Ky., SC 20.

able to name to the bench. Within two and a half years after the defeat of the Court proposal, the President had appointed five of the nine justices: Black, Stanley Reed, Felix Frankfurter, William O. Douglas, and Frank Murphy.

This new Court—the "Roosevelt Court" as it was called—ruled favorably on every one of the New Deal laws whose constitutionality was challenged. It expanded the commerce power and the spending power so greatly that it soon became evident that there was almost no statute for social welfare or the regulation of business that the Court would not uphold. While the Court had once held that the national government lacked the power to regulate even major industries, because it said these industries were not in interstate commerce, the Court now extended the range of the federal government to the most remote businesses. In one case, it held that a farmer was engaged in interstate commerce even when he grew wheat wholly for his own consumption on his own farm.[110]

Since 1937 the Court has not invalidated a single piece of congressional legislation regulating business. Although before 1937 only a few justices were committed to legal realism, after that almost the whole Court moved into that camp and the old doctrines of constitutional fundamentalism lost out. Whereas the beneficiaries of the Court before 1937 had been businessmen and other propertied interests, after 1937 they became the less advantaged groups in America. As early as the first week in June, 1937, *Business Week* was complaining: "The cold fact is that,

---

[110] Wickard *v.* Filburn, 317 U.S. 111 (1942); John W. Davis, Columbia Oral History Collection, Columbia University Library, pp. 165–166.

for all practical purposes, the reorganization of the Court, sought by legislative process, has been accomplished by the ordinary process of court decision."[111] In the fall of 1937, Justice McReynolds grumbled: "The court starts off about as I expected. There is not much to be expected of it by sensible people of the former order."[112] By February, 1938, Frank Gannett was writing: "Since the President now controls the Supreme Court, our only hope lies in influencing the members of Congress."[113] Little wonder that Roosevelt claimed he had lost the battle but won the war.

But there were other respects in which FDR lost the war. The Supreme Court fight spelled the beginning of the end for his New Deal coalition. To be sure, a number of congressmen were probably determined to split with him anyway, and simply used the controversy as an excuse, although even this assigns some importance to the Court battle. Too, the breakup of the coalition resulted, in part, from other developments: the recession of 1937–1938, anxiety over relief spending, resentment at sitdown strikes. But to attempt to explain the rupture of 1937 and ignore the Supreme Court donnybrook is like accounting for the coming of the Civil War without reference to slavery.

The Court struggle had a number of disruptive aspects:

1. It helped blunt the most important drive for social reform in American history and squandered the advantage of Roose-

[111] "What the Court Did to Business," *Business Week*, XVII (June 5, 1937), 17.

[112] James C. McReynolds to Dr. Robert P. McReynolds, Oct. 30, 1937, McReynolds MSS, Alderman Library, University of Virginia, Charlottesville, Va.

[113] Frank Gannett to E. A. Dodd, Feb. 5, 1938, Gannett MSS, Box 16.

velt's triumph in 1936. In the spring of 1937, one observer noted: "Congress has been completely addled by the President's court proposal." The controversy, he added, had resulted "in the sidetracking of much useful legislation that otherwise might have been put through."[114] By the time the session sputtered to an end in "spasms of bitterness" in late August, it had been, as the *New York Times* commented, the "stormiest and least productive in recent years."[115] At the close of the "sock-Roosevelt" session, one reporter wrote: "Tonight the political 'master minds' of the capital gathering over their cups in relaxed reminiscence of the historic events of the last seven months, were mulling over one question: 'How did the President slide so far—so fast?' "[116] The Court struggle helped weld together a bipartisan coalition of anti-New Deal senators who dealt Roosevelt a series of rebuffs at the special session of Congress in the autumn of 1937 and at the regular session in 1938.[117] By the spring of 1938, the prospects for reform had diminished perceptibly, and for the next quarter of a century the advocates of social change would rarely win anything but minor successes in Congress.

2. It deeply divided the Democratic Party. In state after state,

[114] Francis P. Miller to Herbert Claiborne Pell, Apr. 1, 1937, Pell MSS, FDRL, Box 8.

[115] *The New York Times,* Aug. 22, 1937.

[116] Blair Moody in Detroit *News,* Aug. 21, 1937, Blair Moody Scrapbooks, Michigan Historical Collections.

[117] For a well-researched analysis, see James T. Patterson, *Congressional Conservatism and the New Deal* (Lexington, Ky., 1967). The seeds of the coalition had been planted before the Court message. Ralph Flanders to Warren Austin, Jan. 19, 1937, Flanders MSS, Carnegie Library, Syracuse University, Syracuse, N.Y., Box 20.

the Court squabble precipitated factional wars. In Massachusetts, the governor opposed the plan; his auditor and his attorney general favored it.[118] In Montana, the struggle triggered a primary contest between Senator Wheeler and a rival.[119] In numerous states—Indiana, Missouri, New Jersey, Ohio, Rhode Island, South Carolina, Texas, Utah, West Virginia—each of the two Democratic senators pursued a diametrically opposite course on the bill.

Not only did the fight itself open wounds in the party, but it led to a series of later episodes, notably the purge campaign of 1938, which rubbed salt in the wounds. Some of the congressmen who broke with Roosevelt in 1937 were never to give him the same degree of loyalty they had in his first term, and others who were already disaffected soon helped forge a bipartisan anti-New Deal coalition. In April, Senator Bailey observed blandly: "I feel that the President made a mistake, but I am not disposed to criticise him or complain of him. He is on one side and I am on another, but the whole thing will pass." Less than four months later Bailey was writing: "We are engaged in a great battle in America. Do not be deceived about this. The lines are drawn. The issues are clear. Those who are not with us are against us. . . . Men must stand up now. The fight is not over. We have broken down the first big attack, but the attack will be

[118] Springfield *Republican,* Mar. 14, 1937, clipping, David I. Walsh Scrapbooks.

[119] Richard T. Ruetten, "Showdown in Montana, 1938," *Pacific Northwest Quarterly,* LIV (January, 1963), 19–29. I am indebted to Professor Reutten for permission to read his excellent unpublished study of Wheeler.

made on many lines and ultimately there will be another attack on the Court. The socialistic forces of America are not confined to the Socialistic Party."[120]

3. Because of the Court dispute, Roosevelt lost that overwhelming middle class support he had mobilized in the 1936 campaign. Discord over the President's plan, coupled with other events, ended the brief era of great Democratic majorities. An attorney from Lake Charles, Louisiana, wrote: "I voted for President Roosevelt in both elections but would not have done so had he announced his intention to destroy the independence of the judiciary. These are the sentiments of everyone in this City that I have spoken to."[121] A Miami woman protested to a Florida congressman:

"Neither I, nor any of my friends who voted for him, gave him a mandate to destroy the independence of the court, nor of congress.

"I have actually lost faith in his honesty."[122]

A trade unionist from New York confided: "As a member of the Newspaper Guild of America, I have supported the President in the past, because of his humanitarian aims and his attitude toward organized labor. But his present effort to undermine the independence of the Judiciary has destroyed my confidence in his judgment."[123] In North Carolina, a former law school dean told

---

[120] Josiah Bailey to Jas. R. Morris, Apr. 22, 1937; Bailey to Julian Miller, Aug. 4, 1937, Bailey MSS, Duke University Library, Political file.

[121] J. E. Bass to John Overton, Feb. 24, 1937, Overton MSS, Box 2.

[122] Helen St. Clair to Joe Hendricks, Apr. 17, 1937, Hendricks MSS, Box 2.

[123] Walter Parkes to Theodore Green, Apr. 6, 1937, Green MSS, Box 34.

Senator Bailey: "I was an enthusiastic supporter of Roosevelt last November. If an election was held tomorrow, I would not vote for him."[124]

4. The Court issue produced divisions among reformers of many types. It separated Senator Wheeler from labor supporters in Montana and resulted in a breach between Wheeler and the Administration that was never closed.[125] One of Roosevelt's lieutenants observed, "I've always granted to every man the right to his own opinions. . . . But to find Burt in the front ranks of those who were piously upholding the sanctity of the Supreme Court . . . well, that was really a sight to make the angels weep!"[126] In Minnesota, the controversy sundered the Farmer-Labor Party; many Farmer-Laborites were angered by the opposition of Senator Henrik Shipstead to the bill. The president of an organization of "independent" Minnesota lawyers wrote him: "Fake liberals are through[,] Shipstead; so is Burton K. Wheeler. Wait and see."[127] It alienated the publisher of *The Nation* from his editors;

[124] N. Y. Gulley to Josiah Bailey, Mar. 17, 1937, Bailey MSS, Political file. See also William F. Riley to Clyde Herring, July 7, 1937, Riley MSS, Box 1; Martha Washburn Allin to Henry Teigan, Feb. 13, 1937, Teigan MSS, Box 14; B. Agee Bowles to Carter Glass, Mar. 30, 1937, Glass MSS, Alderman Library, University of Virginia, Box 377.

[125] William Brockway to Burton Wheeler, May 15, 1937, Theodore Green MSS, Box 33.

[126] Frank Walker, "My Thoughts on President Roosevelt's Supreme Court Plan," Walker MSS, University of Notre Dame, Notre Dame, Ind.

[127] Albert J. Stafne to Henrik Shipstead, July 23, 1937, Shipstead MSS, Minnesota Historical Society, Box 1. A Minnesota newspaper observed: "The Minnesota Farmer-Labor split was adding evidence of the havoc the court issue is working in party lines and in other previous congressional groupings." Duluth *Herald,* May 13, 1937, clipping, Shipstead MSS, Vol. 22.

split Dr. Townsend from officers of his old age pension organization; and cut off old-line reformers like John Haynes Holmes and Oswald Garrison Villard from the main body of the New Dealers.

5. It undermined the bipartisan support for the New Deal. Many of the Republican progressives had become growingly apprehensive of the men around Roosevelt. The Court issue confirmed them in their suspicions that something alien, something fundamentally illiberal, had been introduced into the reform movement by the New Dealers—that, in the guise of solicitude for the common man, they were actually seeking self-aggrandizement. The President, too, seemed disturbingly eager to concentrate power in Washington. The Republican editor William Allen White, who admired much that the New Deal had achieved, wrote during the Court fight: "I fear him as I fear no other man in our public life."[128] The Court fracas, Hiram Johnson told Raymond Moley, "has forced me into a position of opposition to him, which will widen as the days pass."[129]

6. One tangential result of the Court dispute was that it also helped create distrust for Roosevelt's leadership in foreign policy. Writers frequently likened the Court fight to the League of Nations struggle and compared Hiram Johnson's stand, especially, to that of the original battalion of death. The President's pro-

[128] William Allen White to John Finley, Apr. 29, 1937, White MSS, Box 187.

[129] Hiram Johnson to Raymond Moley, Mar. 13, 1937, Johnson MSS; Edward Dickson to Hiram Johnson, Aug. 17, 1937, Dickson MSS, University of California at Los Angeles Library, Los Angeles, Calif., Box 8, Folder 9.

posal fortified men like Johnson and Wheeler in their misgivings about FDR, for it seemed to reveal what they most deplored about his foreign policy—that it was devious, and that it sought too much power for the Executive.[130]

These multifold misfortunes were a fearful price to pay for the gains Roosevelt achieved. Yet none of these developments should obscure the President's one big success in the Court fight —that he secured the legitimization of the vast expansion of the power of government in American life. The Court struggle speeded the acceptance of a radical change in the role of government and in the reordering of property rights. It also had the probably unanticipated result of the appointment of a Court more interventionist in the field of civil liberties and civil rights. It is not surprising that historians speak of the "Constitutional Revolution of 1937." For in the long history of the Supreme Court, no event had more momentous consequences than Franklin Roosevelt's message of February, 1937.

[130] Hiram Johnson to John Francis Neylan, May 4, 1937, Johnson MSS.

DATE DUE

DATE DUE			
MAR 8 '71			
MAR 17 '71			
APR 6 '71			
APR 20 '71			
MAY 6 '71			
MAY 6 '71			
FEB 15 '72			
GAYLORD			PRINTED IN U.S.A.